ASYMMETRIC
SAILING

ASYMMETRIC
SAILING

Andy Rice

WILEY

John Wiley & Sons Ltd

Wiley Nautical – sharing your passion.

At Wiley Nautical we're passionate about anything that happens in, on or around the water.

Wiley Nautical used to be called Fernhurst Books and was founded by a national and European sailing champion. Our authors are the leading names in their fields with Olympic gold medals around their necks and thousands of sea miles in their wake. Wiley Nautical is still run by people with a love of sailing, motorboating, surfing, diving, kitesurfing, canal boating and all things aquatic.

Visit us online at www.wileynautical.com for offers, videos, podcasts and more.

Contents

Acknowledgements

The Experts

There are many friends and experts whose advice I sought when writing the book, some of them quoted, some of them not. From 20 years of racing in fleets like the Laser 5000, the 49er, International 14 and Musto Skiff, I've had the fortune to race with or against some of the best skiff sailors in the business, and I've badgered them for tips and advice along the way. There isn't room to mention everyone I spoke to, but here's a brief background of some of the experts whose advice crops up in the book.

Glenn Ashby, Olympic medallist from Australia, multiple world champion in a range of multi-hulls and America's Cup winning coach.

Trevor Baylis, a great crew who makes every boat he gets into go faster. He's won the 505, International 14 and 18ft Skiff World Championships.

Mitch Booth, Dutch, Spanish, Australian? I'm not sure which, but he still sounds Aussie to me. Wherever he's from, a great multihull sailor with two Olympic medals and fistful of world titles.

Paul Brotherton, a 49er European Champion from Great Britain, former 470 Olympic representative, and one of the best coaches in the business. He coached the Yngling girls to Olympic gold in Qingdao 2008 and the British 49er team for Weymouth 2012.

Andy Budgen, one of the most talented skiff sailors even if he's not a household name. He's placed 2nd in the 49er Worlds and 18ft Skiffs and coaches many top teams in the 49er class.

Darren Bundock, the most successful small cat sailor ever? Not sure, but this Australian has been there done it, with two Olympic medals and a boatload of multihull world titles in the Tornado and F18 classes, and a few others besides.

Geoff Carveth, one of Britain's biggest names outside the Olympic scene, with two SB20 world titles and many national dinghy titles in all kinds of classes, asymmetrics included.

Derek Clark, a 470 Olympian, America's Cup designer, and the driving force behind a number of skiff projects including the Laser 5000 and more recently the Rebel Skiff, which features in many of the photo sequences in the book.

Chris Draper, 49er World Champion and Olympic medallist, and in recent years an Extreme Sailing Series champion and America's Cup skipper in the ultra-fast AC45 multihulls.

Dave Hivey, one of Britain's up and coming talents on the small boat scene, having won national titles in the highly competitive RS200 and RS400 fleets.

Brian Hutchinson, known as the go-to guy in the Melges fleet. A Melges 24 World Champion from the USA, Brian's knowledge of asymmetrics and sportsboats knows no bounds.

Steve Irish, a 420 World Champion who moved into asymmetrics and won the RS800 Nationals. Steve is in great demand as a full-time coach to Britain's Olympic and youth squads.

Stevie Morrison, 49er and Fireball World Champion from Britain, with a great natural flair for making a boat go fast.

Chris Nicholson, dominated the 18ft Skiff circuit back in its professional heyday, then won three 49er World Championships. These days Chris makes his living as a skipper in the Volvo Ocean Race.

Charlie Ogletree, Olympic silver medallist in the Tornado, and the only sailor ever to have trimmed an asymmetric sail at an Olympic Games, going upwind!

Richard Parslow, a Fireball World Champion, and my coach when I was in the British 49er squad. A goal-setting expert extraordinaire.

Rick Perkins, a Fireball National Champion, but more importantly for this book, a Musto Skiff National Champion.

Frances Peters, ISAF Youth World Champion in the 29er class. She won the girls' fleet but she probably would have beaten the boys too. A rising star in skiff sailing.

Mari Shepherd, a top 29er crew, and never afraid of a new challenge, such as when we put her out in the Rebel Skiff for our windy photoshoot.

Chris Simon, rules expert and consultant who has worked at every level of the sport, including the Olympics, America's Cup and Volvo Ocean Race.

Photographers

Thanks to the photographers and organisations who were kind enough to allow the use of their work for this book.

Ingrid Abery, for her excellent cover shot (www.hotcapers.com)

Fiona Brown, for some great Melges 24 shots (www.fionabrown.phanfare.com)

Brian Carlin, wonderful SB20 photos (CubeImages.com)

GBR International 14 Class, with special thanks to Andrew Penman (gbr.international14.org)

Roland and Nahid Gaebler, for their Tornado images (www.teamgaebler.de)

Natalie Hilton, for her Musto Skiff photos

Gunnar Larsen, for the Nacra catamaran photos (www.nacrasailing.com)

Paul Manning, for photos from the archive of the Musto Skiff Class Association (www.mustoskiff.com)

Chris Simon, for his brilliant illustrations for the Rules chapter

Thanks for the boats

Alice Moore for the loan of her RS200 for a photoshoot at my sailing club, Stokes Bay Sailing Club

Derek Clark for driving the photo boat and the loan of his Rebel Skiff, and to **Andy Budgen, Dave Hivey** and **Mari Shepherd** for getting very wet in the making of those photos.

About the Author

Andy Rice has won championships from both ends of a skiff, winning a 49er national championship as a helm and International 14 Europeans and Prince of Wales Weeks as a crew. He has sailed with a number of top sailors over the years, including Olympic medallists John Merricks, Ian Walker and Simon Hiscocks.

As a sailing journalist, he has reported on every major event from the Olympics to the America's Cup, the Volvo Ocean Race and the Vendée Globe. He writes for many racing-oriented magazines including Seahorse, Yachts and Yachting, Yachting World, Boat International and Sailing World.

Together with James Boyd, editor of the news website TheDailySail.com, Andy runs Sailing Intelligence, a specialist marine media agency. Andy's passion is for asking great sailors what makes them tick, and finding out why they're so fast. That was the basis of writing Asymmetric Sailing, and is also the basis of SailJuice.com, Andy's online treasure trove of top sailboat racing tips.

Learn more about Asymmetric Sailing

Go to www.wileynautical.com/asymmetric for more tips, plus interviews, videos and further links.

INTRODUCTION

Who will benefit from this book?

I'm going to assume that you're already familiar with the sport of sailing, and that you've done a bit of racing too. This book is not aimed at the novice, although it is aimed at sailors who may never have sailed boats with asymmetric spinnakers before. It is hard to write a book that will appeal to all types of asymmetric sailor, but in this book you'll discover I've interviewed a range of experts across a spectrum of sailing boats powered by asymmetric sails.

We've got tips on how to get the best out of:

- small dinghies like the RS200 and RS400,
- high performance skiffs such as 49ers and International 14s,
- high performance multihulls such as Tornados and Formula 18 catamarans, and
- sportsboats such as the Melges 24 and SB20.

Competitive racing in the Melges 24 fleet

Even if your particular boat isn't directly covered in this book, I really hope you get some great tips from some of the experts we've gathered together, and that you'll be able to carry over some of the hot tips into your own asymmetric sailing.

Asymmetric Sails + Apparent Wind = Fast and Fun

To sail successfully with an asymmetric spinnaker – or gennaker – requires you to start understanding what apparent wind is. Apparent wind is the wind that is generated by the boat moving forwards. It's the same wind as you feel when you stick your hand out the window of a car when the car is moving, or it's the wind in your face when you are cycling. It's artificially generated wind, so you can feel apparent wind even when there is no true wind blowing at all.

Understanding the effect of apparent wind is crucial to sailing with asymmetric spinnakers, but it will also help improve your understanding of all types of sailing. It's easy to think that, on a simple singlehanded boat like an Optimist, Topper or Laser, you run downwind just by presenting the sail to the wind and getting blown along, without any flow across the sail. Indeed that's how most club sailors do run downwind in a Laser, but ask an Olympic standard sailor

Harnessing apparent wind is the key to fast sailing in asymmetrics

how they steer the Laser downwind, and they're always doing angles, always with flow across the sail. They may be sailing a greater distance, but the increased efficiency by having flow across the sail more than makes up for the extra distance.

Unlike a conventional, symmetric spinnaker or the mainsail on a singlehander, the asymmetric spinnaker cannot function without flow across the sail. It is absolutely reliant on wind blowing across the sail. But once you understand this, and that by combining the true wind with the apparent wind generated by your forward motion, then you will discover that you can achieve much greater boatspeeds. Many asymmetric dinghies and multihulls are capable of travelling at least as fast as wind speed and in some extreme cases such as the AC45 America's Cup catamarans, travelling in excess of three times true windspeed is achievable.

One of the fun by-products of asymmetrics is that for the reasons just given, you can't sail dead downwind – or at least it's very slow and inefficient to do so. Because you want to maximise the apparent wind, you are always sailing angles downwind. Now the run starts to feel similar to an upwind leg, where any sailor knows that it is impossible to sail directly to the windward mark. Well, to some extent the same is true with an asymmetric boat. You have to sail angles, and that makes for a much more tactically interesting and challenging scenario.

AC45 America's Cup catamarans can travel up to three times the speed of the wind

However, an asymmetric sail's inability to sail dead downwind is not always a good thing. For example, if you are sailing in confined waters such as in a river or a stream, or you are running close to a shore against an adverse tide, you don't want to have to drive out into stronger tide. So there are times when you notice the limitations of an asymmetric sail; but most of the time – and certainly in open water – the benefits of an asymmetric far out weigh the benefits of a symmetrical sail. With the asymmetric's superior ability to generate its own wind, it encourages you to start looking for gusts, to look around for the strongest wind on the water. In a high performance boat, finding one knot more of true wind speed can help generate as much as two knots more of actual speed through the water.

So there are very good tactical and strategic reasons for sailing with an asymmetric. In many ways it makes the game more difficult and more challenging but, ultimately, more rewarding when you start to appreciate the tactical and strategic rules of asymmetric sailing.

One of the other benefits of the asymmetric is that, by and large, it is much easier to hoist, gybe and lower an asymmetric spinnaker than a conventional symmetrical spinnaker. It's why, over the past ten years, the majority of beginners and family-oriented boats have come fitted with asymmetric spinnakers rather than anything else.

You have a bowsprit, sometimes fixed but quite often retractable. On many modern dinghies and catamarans, the gennaker halyard is also connected to a set of blocks which pull the bowsprit out at the same time. So one person pulls just one rope which launches the pole and hoists the sail in one movement. Compare this with a spinnaker where typically, on a two-person boat, it might be the helm who's busy hoisting the spinnaker to the top of the mast while the crew is busy connecting one end of the pole to the guy, connecting the centre of the pole to the topping lift, and connecting the inboard end of the pole to the loop on the mast and then setting the spinnaker guy to the right place.

Some people enjoy the challenge of that and, for many sailors, it is one of the fun aspects of crewing. Some would argue that there is a lot of skill in how you get the best out of a spinnaker.

Handling a gennaker is more straightforward than a traditional spinnaker

The author sailing a Devoti D-1 at Lake Garda

The other side of it is that it is much easier to learn how to sail with a gennaker, because you just pull one rope and you're away. In fact, one friend asked me how I could find enough information to fill a whole book on the subject. Yes, at its very simplest, you pull in a gennaker sheet until the sail stops flapping. That's it! End of book!

But the reality is that while gennakers are very forgiving sails to use, they also tend to be attached to boats that are very demanding to sail and race. This book is dedicated to helping you get to grips with the wider game of asymmetric sailing and racing. In the process of researching this subject I've spoken to some of the very best in the business. After almost 20 years of racing boats at world championship level – such as 49ers, International 14s and SB20s – I thought I knew most of what there was to know, but the asymmetric spinnaker is still a fairly new innovation in the history of sailing and we're learning new tricks all the time. This book condenses the very best of what I've learned up to now. I hope you enjoy it, and that you find good, solid tips that you can apply to your own asymmetric sailing.

Andy Rice, July 2012

P.S. Throughout the book I refer to 'asymmetric spinnakers', 'asymmetrics', 'gennakers' (half genoa/half spinnaker), and 'kites'. They are all one and the same thing. I try to avoid the term 'spinnaker', reserving that for conventional, symmetrically-shaped spinnakers.

CHAPTER 1

GETTING STARTED

Choosing the Right Boat

It's not within the scope of this book to ask you too many questions about what kind of boat you plan to sail. Because asymmetrics come in many different shapes and sizes, it's difficult to hand out any specific advice, but I just want you to be sure that you've thought about the following factors:

Ability

Do you have the ability to sail the boat competently? Or, let's put it another way, do you have the potential? Now, I know sailors in their 50s and 60s who handle the 18-foot Skiff and Musto Skiff very competently, and asymmetric boats don't get much harder than that. Ian Renilson is still knocking in top ten finishes at Musto Skiff World Championships well into his 50s, although he is a former Contender World Champion. But Ian, like most other Musto Skiff sailors, did a lot of capsizing and swimming before he reached a certain level of competence. Are

The 18-foot Skiff is great fun if you know what you're doing, but it will bite you if you don't!

you prepared to do the same? If so, great! If not, then maybe you want something a bit more stable and easier to handle.

Team

Are you going to be sailing in a team boat? If so, how much can you rely on your team mate(s) to show up on a regular basis? Better to agree on the goals and the schedule for the year before you put down your hard cash on a boat.

Budget

Do you have the money, not just for the boat, but for its upkeep and maintenance? If you're racing a boat where you expect to be doing a lot of capsizing and putting the equipment through quite a bit of abuse while you drag yourself up the learning curve, then it may be better to do your learning on a well-sorted secondhand boat. Even better if you can get the seller to throw in a day's coaching to help you get to grips with the basics. It's also a great way to check that the boat you're buying is working properly and that you haven't been sold a pup.

To sail a high-performance boat well, team mates need to share the same goals and ambitions

Local fleet

Is there a local fleet at a nearby sailing club, or a good racing circuit that you can get involved in? While any new boat is exciting to sail initially, the novelty will eventually wear off. But it's the racing and the camaraderie that will keep you interested. So give this factor some serious thought before deciding which boat to sail.

Apparent Wind Sailing

Got to get up to get down. . .

One of the difficult things to get your head around when you're discovering asymmetric sailing for the first time is the idea that if you want to get downwind you need to head up first. In planing conditions, if you want to get the bow pointing as low as possible downwind and make the best VMG (Velocity Made Good) to the next mark at the bottom of the course, then the way to do that

To create your apparent wind, first you need to luff up to build the speed

initially is actually to head up as high away from the wind as you can. Unless you do this, you're not really apparent wind sailing, you are just wafting downwind with the breeze and the gennaker will be caught behind the mainsail and the jib, and will never get a chance to fill properly. So, if you're new to this, the first thing to do is to head up perhaps more than you think you need to, and get the air flowing across the gennaker from luff to leech and drafting out the back of the sail.

Once you do that, the apparent wind will kick in and start building on itself. As the apparent wind increases, it also moves forward and you need to sheet on the gennaker and the mainsail to compensate. And, if it's windy, you'll need to hike out as hard as possible to counteract the increase in power. In strong winds you'll find those who hike out hardest actually end up sailing lowest and deepest towards the leeward mark. At first it doesn't seem to make sense. After all, in most sailing you sit in to sail lower, but not in an asymmetric when you've got the power of apparent wind on your side.

How low can you go?

In light to medium airs, when there isn't enough wind to get the boat planing, then it's about sailing as low as possible before you experience a massive drop-off in flow across the sails. Where sailing dead downwind is an option in non-asymmetric boats, it's never an option with

MELGES 24s trying to 'soak' low in non-planing conditions

asymmetrics. You always need to sail angles downwind, and in light to medium conditions the trick is finding out just how low you can go.

On a keelboat you may have electronic GPS equipment which you can use to help determine your best VMG downwind. On a dinghy or a small multihull, you don't have that luxury so you have to develop a feel for when you think the boat is travelling at the optimum VMG downwind. Quite often you can't really work this out until you start racing other boats, when you can compare yourself to others nearby. In marginal planing conditions you'll find there are those who like pushing high and sailing extra distance for the extra speed, while there are those who like really running deep and going slower, but sailing a shorter distance to the next mark.

Both those extremes have their place, and sometimes it pays to do a little bit of each. A lot of the time, the decision that you make about whether to sail in high, medium or low

Two International 14s sailing in very different modes

mode is based on the tactics of where the boats around you are, and where you're aiming for next. It is also based on where you think the best breeze is. Sometimes, when you're in a nice but narrow line of breeze, it pays to sail low to stay in it as long as possible. The temptation can be to head up, get on the plane and sail really fast – only to sail yourself out of the breeze line.

So it's really important to be able to sail in all these modes. We'll address this in Chapter 7, Boat Speed. And it's also important to know how and when to apply these modes on the race course, which we'll address in Chapter 8, Racing: Strategy and Tactics.

Getting to Grips with Asymmetrics

Former ISAF Youth World Champion in the 29er, Frances Peters, looks back at her move into asymmetrics from conventional dinghies:

"It was a big transition to make at first, because suddenly you're sailing big angles downwind. There's so much more to be gained and lost, so it was a big mental transition and you had to start thinking about it from a new perspective. Upwind we get used to watching pressure [the wind] coming down and sailing to the pressure and sailing on the lifted tack. You've got to start thinking in a similar way downwind. But it's another perspective downwind because you're actually sailing away from the pressure, so you've got to watch where the pressure's going and you've got to try to find ways to stay in the pressure as it moves. Equally it's easy to ignore shifts downwind and you should try and pay more attention to them as well.

I've found that having got some experience in asymmetric sailing, going back into a symmetrical conventional spinnaker or a boat without a spinnaker at all, it really helped my sailing. It really made me think a lot more about what was going on around me, and there's so much to be gained and lost downwind as well as upwind. Before asymmetric sailing, I used to think that places weren't really gained or lost downwind and that actually it didn't really make much of a difference which way you went. But as you start sailing in asymmetrics, you realise that there's so much else going on around you. It highlights the difference in pressure and shifts across the course, and although it's not as obvious in other types of sailing, it still applies. Sailing asymmetrics makes you much more aware of the possibilities downwind."

Getting the Basics Right

How is your boat rigged: bag or chute?

If you're using a boat with a spinnaker chute then it's the crew who tends to do all the hoisting in a two-handed boat. The helm's chief job is to steer the boat so that it's upright and stable and gives the crew plenty of opportunity to hoist the spinnaker without worrying about helping to keep the boat upright.

With a boat with a chute, you might want to share out the job of hoisting the gennaker, as there are more ropes to pull. So, for example, in the Laser 5000, a typical routine would be for the helm to pull up the spinnaker halyard while the crew pulls out the pole and the tack line. So it's a matter of dividing up the workflow in such a way that you get your gennaker up and pulling in the shortest amount of time after the windward mark.

Despite the enormous sail, the 18-foot skiff gennaker is launched and retrieved into a bag

In a boat with three or more crew, such as a Melges 24 or SB20, then you can divide up the workload even more. So in the case of a three-person SB20, the typical work pattern would be:

- Helm continues to steer while taking the mainsheet from the middle man.
- Forward hand goes to leeward to prepare the gennaker by opening up the bag. He then pulls out the bowsprit. At the helmsman's command the forward hand hoists the gennaker and cleats it off.
- While the forward hand is hoisting the gennaker, the middle man pulls the tack line until the tack reaches the end of the bowsprit. He then moves straight to the kite sheet (taking it from the helm if the helm has already picked it up) and gets the kite set while the forward hand sets the jib and tidies the cockpit and the kite halyard in particular.

Rigging the Gennaker

When you rig the gennaker, make sure you get it right before you go afloat! I can guarantee that at some point in your asymmetric sailing career, you will forget this simple advice. Some lessons you have to learn for yourself, and believe me, there are few more embarrassing or

Have a set routine for rigging the boat, and you'll avoid foul-ups on the water

painful that having to re-rig the gennaker out on the water. It's not easy, and it often results in a capsize. You can remind me of this fact the next time you see me up on the foredeck of my Musto Skiff!

If you launch from bags, as with a B14 or an 18-foot Skiff, then at least all you have to do is tie three corners to the correct rope. But for the sake of simplicity and avoiding silly errors, make sure you write 'Tack', 'Clew' and 'Head' on the correct corners. And I'd tie them on in that order too, although this isn't too critical. One reason for doing this is for rigging up on a windy day, when you don't want to have the kite blowing around the dinghy park and potentially capsizing your boat. Having the names written on the corners means you can have the kite stuffed in the bag and still tie on the corners without exposing too much sail to the wind.

Now, if you launch from a chute, which is the norm for most asymmetric dinghies and small catamarans, then you have the added complication of a retrieval line, which is basically the other end of the halyard because it's one continuous line. The retrieval line makes it much more possible to create tangles and to get it wrong if you're not careful with your rigging procedure. It also makes it much harder to re-rig it on the water if you get it wrong, so it's particularly important to make sure that you've got your rigging correct with a chute style of boat.

There are different ways of doing it, but my favourite way of rigging a gennaker on an International 14 or a 49er for example, is to:

- tie the tack first, with the bowsprit retracted into the boat;
- loop the kite sheets through the clew and reeve the port sheet through the port-hand ratchet block on the boat;
- pull the foot of the sail tight so that you know there's no tangle. I do this on the port side of the boat on the 14 because this is the side where the kite hoists from;
- take the retrieval line (already threaded through the spinnaker sock) and run it underneath the foot of the sail, and then run it through the bottom retrieval patch near the foot;
- depending on whether you've got a one-, two- or three-patch retrieval system on your kite, make sure that the halyard is going through all the correct patches, and then tie the end of the retrieval line off to the top retrieval patch;
- take the other gennaker sheet that runs around the starboard side of the boat, take this starting from the clew, and run it along the side of the boat *inside* the gennaker, making sure it goes over the *top* of the retrieval line, runs around the forestay and then back down the other side of the boat through the ratchet block;
- tie off your gennaker sheets in the middle of the cockpit, and
- tie the halyard on to the head of the kite.

The reason for attaching the halyard last is so that if the wind does catch the sail while you're rigging it, you're not going to get it filling and flying out from the top of the mast, potentially capsizing the boat and causing damage while you are on the shore. So the gennaker halyard is always the last thing to be tied on and then you're ready to fully retract the kite into the chute and that should make sure that you don't have any tangles. If it's windy you can pull most of the sail into the chute before you attach the halyard.

If the winds are light, and you don't think it's going to cause any harm to the boat, then take the opportunity to double check your rigging. Hoist the gennaker to the top of the mast and make

ADDING A SPACER KNOT TO THE RETRIEVAL LINE

If you've got a kite with two or three patches, then the sail can bunch up at the chute mouth as you're pulling it back into the boat during a kite drop. This can sometimes create extra friction and effort for the crew at a crucial point in the race. One way to avoid this is to thread a plastic ball on to the retrieval line which sits between two of the patches. If you tie a figure-of-eight stopper knot or a long bowline, and create a gap of, say, 10cm between the patches, this will help avoid the bunching effect as you haul the kite back into the chute.

Yellow retrieval line is tied with a long bowline to keep the patches apart as they go into the chute

sure that all the sheets are running clear. If the winds are strong, the chances are you won't get an opportunity to do that, which means that when you get out on the race course, unless it really is extremely windy, you want to check that you rigged the gennaker correctly as early as possible before the start of the race. If by any chance you have made a mistake, you at least give yourself the maximum time to put it right. But good luck!

Health & Safety

There's some safety gear and clothing you might want to take with you, particularly if you're sailing a high performance boat for the first time. Take a knife, in fact take two. I keep one in my buoyancy aid tied to a lanyard, and I keep a diver's knife on the back bar of the Musto Skiff. It doesn't happen often, but every few years there is a story of a sailor who got tangled up with the rigging or caught under the boat, and a knife might just have made the difference to whether they lived or drowned.

Knife. Take a knife, and wash it in fresh water after every time you sail so that it stays sharp and ready for action.

Spares. Take a shackle key, some spare shackles and a spare piece of rope. You'll be surprised how often you need them, and how much easier life becomes when you have them at the ready.

Wear gloves. If you're sailing an asymmetric boat properly, you're moving sheets all the time, and that can wear out your skin really quickly. If you're steering a 49er or other skiffs where the crew is playing the mainsheet upwind, then you might get away without gloves, but pretty much every other job on an asymmetric boat requires gloves.

Helmets. I've never worn one but I've certainly thought about it, particularly for those days where I'm out on the open sea in my Musto Skiff by myself. When you're learning and expecting a bit of crash and burn, a helmet will give you a lot more confidence to take risks. It will help speed up your learning curve.

Foot loops. These are vital bits of kit on high performance trapeze boats, and can be as simple as a piece of hose pipe with some rope running through the centre, to ready-made windsurfer footstraps to specially made sailing footloops. It's really down to personal preference. Some are designed to give way if they're subjected to a lot of force. The idea is that, if you have a

Builders' gloves are cheap and have great grip

Footloops should be stiff enough to stand upright for easy access

big tumble, the foot loop detaches before it causes damage to your foot or ankle. It doesn't happen very often, but people have occasionally been known to break an ankle when they get their foot stuck after falling off the boat in a capsize. So it's important to get some footloops that you have confidence in using.

Going Sailing for the First Time

Tempting as it might be to launch your new boat the first time, be sure to pick the right conditions, particularly if you've chosen a boat that is more high performance than you've been used to. Just bear in mind your level of experience and don't give yourself too much to do the first time you go out sailing.

If you possibly can, find someone who's already got experience in the boat to go sailing with you the first time. It will massively shorten your learning curve, and could help you avoid some costly errors.

A great shortcut to better boathandling from day one, is to do some shore drills. Tie the boat down very securely to the shore – on its trolley or on some tyres – and anchor the boat side to side to the ground so that it's firm enough that you can actually sit on board the boat and you can walk around it, and sit down from one gunnel to the other. If it's a trapeze boat, you want to be able to trapeze off the side of it and you can work out a lot of your routines, your foot movements and your hand movements without having the added challenge of worrying about keeping the boat upright. If you're going to be dry-land trapezing, tie an anchor rope around the mast at hounds height and secure it side to side, so that you can get out on the trapeze knowing you're not going to capsize the boat on top of you!

Now, you might think that you look like a beginner doing this, and maybe you do! But some of the best sailors, including top Olympic 49er sailors like Olympic medallist and world champion Chris Draper, taught themselves how to sail the 49er like this, by learning their foot movements and hand

Double-check everything before you go afloat

movements and doing all that stuff on shore many, many times so that the way that they wanted to do it became the way that they automatically did it when they went out sailing. It's a great way of ingraining good habits from the very start.

Once again, the process becomes even more valuable if you can find somebody who already has more experience of sailing that kind of boat than you do. So, get them to show you what they do, invite them to go for a walk around the boat and show you the different things that they do through various manoeuvres. It's also a good way of practising and improving your sailing on a day when there's no wind, or there's too much wind to safely go sailing. A good way of making use of what otherwise would be wasted sailing time.

Once you feel that you've got those drills for all the various manoeuvres worked out – the main ones being tacking, gybing, hoisting, dropping the gennaker – then pick a day, a light to medium air's day to go sailing for the first time. Again, if you've got the option to sail with someone with some experience as opposed to maybe the person who's going to be your regular crew or helm, then take the experienced person because you'll learn so much more about how to do things right first go. You'll probably end up breaking less gear, capsizing less, feeling more confident in the boat much sooner if you've learnt from someone else who's been through the learning curve already. You can then take that experience with you back into the boat when you start sailing with your regular sailing partner.

One of the most important things that you need to be able to do safely, is to hoist and, particularly, lower the sails. That should be your first drill, to hoist the gennaker, making sure that it's rigged correctly once it's been hoisted, setting the gennaker and then lowering the gennaker again. Once you've done that then you can try experimenting with some gybes, sailing the boat at different angles with the gennaker hoisted trying a very deep run and trying a tight reach provided it's not too windy, just getting comfortable with how the gennaker works and how it responds to different sailing directions.

Safe Launch and Recovery

Launching from a lee shore

One of the most challenging parts of sailing high-performance boats is launching them off the shore, particularly if the wind is blowing directly on shore, the dreaded 'lee shore'.

Have a set routine for launching, and give yourself more time than you think you need

If you're sailing a doublehanded boat, then the crew (or whoever's biggest and strongest of the two) should hold the boat in the water by the windward shroud, while the other sailor takes the trolley back to the beach, and then hops into the boat to get the board and rudder down as much as possible in the depth of water available.

Then, as the crew gets ready to hop into the boat, the helm should have tiller in hand and get the jib half-sheeted, ready to pull the bow away from the wind. As the crew jumps in, avoid the temptation to get away from the shore as quickly as possible – i.e. don't try and point into the wind. This will almost certainly stall the boat and you'll most likely blow back on to the shore.

Instead, get the jib pulling and feel what the forces are on the rudder. Only pull in the mainsail if you feel lee-helm in the rudder, i.e. you are having to push the rudder away. On the other

Musto Skiffs launching from a lee shore. Note the windward heel to keep the boat sailing in a straight line with half board and rudder down

hand if you're feeling weather helm, pull on some more jib and heel the boat slightly to windward. All the while the crew wants to gauge the depth of water and get the board fully down as soon as possible. The same goes for the helm and the rudder, but don't do this at the expense of losing control of the boat. Keeping the boat going in a straight line and avoiding the stall remains the highest priority until you are safely away from the shore.

Launching from a windward shore

If you're launching from a windward shore, things get easier, although if you're sailing a high-powered skiff then the bear-away can, in itself, be quite a challenge in strong winds. In this case, get the rudder half-way down, but launch with the daggerboard fully up. Although the boat will be slightly tippy, provided you're aware of this fact you'll be fine, and you'll drift sideways out into deeper water. Then, once you're away from the shore, put the daggerboard in, get the rudder fully down, and then start sailing.

Landing on a lee shore

If you're coming into a lee shore, it's often worth dropping the mainsail before you come in. Do this at least 50 metres off shore – possibly more, depending on how long you think it will take to get the main down and safely stowed in the cockpit. If it's particularly windy, you might even want to furl, lower or unhook the jib from the sheet, as you'll be amazed how quickly you approach the shore even with a small amount of sail area.

Landing on a windward shore

As you get within jumping out point of the shore, raise the board and rudder halfway, and the crew should be ready to jump out and get wet at least up to the waist, possibly up to the neck if you've misjudged your approach! But generally this is simplest of all the launching and recovery manoeuvres.

CHAPTER 2

STANDARD MOVES

F irst let's look at all the standard moves you need to know in order to get around the race course. We'll cover some of the more fancy stuff later. Mainly we'll be focused on using the asymmetric sail downwind, but we do need to know how to manoeuvre the boat all the way round the course. So before we head downwind, let's take a brief look at tacking upwind.

Tacking

Tacking on most asymmetric boats is not radically different to any other boat of similar ilk. There's not much that need's altering on a hiking boat, a keelboat or a multihull.

But lightweight skiffs, particularly with self-tacking jibs, do require some thought about technique. Firstly, aim for a flat boat throughout the manoeuvre. Don't try to roll tack the boat, as you'll never cope with the power and acceleration you already have. When the battens on a fully-battened rig pop through to the new tack, you already have a power surge to cope with and, if anything, you want to exit a tack slightly heeled to windward so that you come upright as the battens pop.

Andy Budgen and Mari Shepherd come off the trapeze as they start to tack the Rebel Skiff *(Continued)*

Andy and Mari move through the boat in unison, matching their speed of movement to the speed of the boat tacking, maintaining a flat boat throughout the turn. . . *(Continued)*

As they exit the tack, the crew picks up the mainsheet with her aft (now her left) hand, while the helm allows a little windward heel, ensuring the boat won't stall and luff back head to wind. . . *(Continued)*

With the boat flat throughout the tack, and safely on the new heading, Andy and Mari can take their time getting hooked up on to their trapeze wires knowing that they're safely through the tack.

If you've got a self-tacking jib, most likely it will be the crew taking the main through the tack. If it's off-the-boom sheeting, most crews prefer to pass the mainsheet behind their back as they move through the boat.

For the helm, the most important thing is to steer slowly but consistently through the tack on to the new course. Don't slow down too much, or else the boat will lose momentum and stall. But don't oversteer, otherwise you'll struggle to cope with too much power, especially if the jib is still sheeted in hard. Easing the jib sheet a few inches before the tack will give you a bit more room for error until you get the hang of the tack.

Wire-to-wire tacking

Wire-to-wire tacking looks great, and it's not as hard to do as it might look. If you've got your handles set to the right height, then you can hang on a straight arm, which doesn't require too much strength. If you're sailing a twin-trapeze boat, it's great if the helm can do this too, but it's not essential, it's just the icing on the cake.

However, it is very useful for the crew to be able to reliably wire-to-wire tack – and gybe for that matter – as it gives the helm a lot of confidence in being able to steer all the way through the manoeuvre on to the new heading, knowing that the weight of the crew will be there to counteract the power surge as the sails fill on the new tack. It makes the manoeuvre a lot more predictable and safer.

With practice, the crew should be able to hook up on the new side while hanging on to the handle and also holding the mainsheet. But, in the early days, it's OK to hand the mainsheet over to the helm until the crew is hooked on and settled.

Some singlehanded trapeze sailors in the RS700 and Musto Skiff like to wire-to-wire tack and gybe, but this is a high-risk option, as there's no second pair of hands to help out if you start struggling to juggle tiller, mainsheet and trapeze handle. Much better to practise a more predictable manoeuvre where you get your body weight on the new rack, settle on the new heading, and then get out on the trapeze.

Gybing Without the Gennaker

One of the benefits of travelling fast downwind with the gennaker is that the force of the wind as you go through the gybe is fairly small, particularly in planing asymmetric boats. Let's say you're sailing in 15 knots of breeze and moving at about 11 knots giving you an apparent wind of 11 knots – so you've only got 4 knots blowing across the deck. The boom will almost float across during the gybe, none of the slamming from one side to the other that you get on slower

Gybing a Devoti D-1 without the gennaker

boats. This means that when you don't have the gennaker, you actually miss that extra speed of going downwind. You're back in the more familiar territory of conventional boats, of having to cope with a much greater force on the boom when the boom gybes.

You still need to be able to know how to gybe without the gennaker, whether it's for the manoeuvres in the pre-start, or if you've been told to take a 360 or a 720 penalty. If you have to do this in a strong breeze, the 'no-gennaker' gybe is about the hardest manoeuvre you can do, so it's well worth practising a drill outside of racing.

The other areas where gybing without the kite can help during a racing situation are at a windward mark where you might want to gybe immediately onto port gybe to get into a fresh line of breeze on that side of the course. Or it might be that there's a raft-up at the leeward gate and you have to get the gennaker down early – in which case you'll have to gybe without it.

There are even extreme situations in 49er world championships where teams have actively decided not to hoist the gennaker because they pretty much know that they're going to capsize on the gybe, whether they're flying the gennaker or not. They take the view that if you're going to capsize, it's going to be quicker to get the boat upright again with just main and jib, and not having to worry about getting the gennaker back in the chute first. So they were going for two-sail gybes and hoping for the best, and if they got through it upright, then that was a bonus.

Gybe with pace

So how do you do it? As with any gybe, the key to a successful no-gennaker gybe is to go into the gybe with as much pace as possible and to maintain that pace as much as possible all the way through the gybe. If you're in a trapezing boat, ideally it means staying on the trapeze for as long as possible on a power reach, sailing as fast as you can with the righting moment available to you. So if you're in a hiking boat, hiking as hard as you can and then as you steer into the gybe, try not to let the main out too much. Because the more that you let the main out, the further you'll have to turn through the breeze when you come out of the manoeuvre on the new gybe.

Sail into the gybe with as much speed as possible, and you have a much better chance of staying upright

Better if you can keep the mainsail two-thirds in and then as the boom starts to swing across you have a bit of mainsheet that you can ease to soften the blow of the boom slamming across. Also, if one of you can grab the boom and haul it across the centreline just before it gybes of its own accord, it reduces the amount of steering required. The problem with waiting for the boom to cross by itself is that you need to steer higher for this to happen, and the higher you sail out of the gybe, the more prone you are to broaching. So, do whatever you can to convince that boom to get across sooner than it would like.

If you're sailing a boat with two or more people, you need to aim to co-ordinate getting your weight from one side to the other with your weight in the middle of the boat for the minimum of time. Move from fully hiking on one gybe to fully hiking on the other gybe as quickly as possible.

In moderate-to-strong winds, you won't need to apply any roll to your gybe. You want to be flat all the way through the manoeuvre, possibly even slightly heeled to leeward on a very high-speed high-wind gybe. If in doubt about how quickly to get your body weight across to the new windward side of the boat, do it sooner than later. Do it too late and the boat will fall in to windward. Do it too early and you'll let the boat heel to leeward and you probably won't make it through the gybe at all, but you'll broach and capsize on the gybe that you were already on. Eight times out of ten, though, the reason why people capsize on windy two-sail gybes is because they've moved their body weight across too late.

If you're sailing a trapeze boat and you've got your teamwork well worked out, the crew should run straight for the new trapeze handle and jump straight out on the new gunnel of the boat. This means the helm can confidently steer high out of the gybe to take advantage of the extra righting moment.

If the crew doesn't manage to take the jib through with them on this manoeuvre and the sail flaps, that's OK. At this stage of such a difficult manoeuvre, crew weight and balance of the boat is more important than setting the sails. You can sort that out after you've safely got through the manoeuvre.

If you're not confident of being able to get a lot of crew weight onto the new side quickly, then the helm needs to steer more of an 'S' shape out of the gybe, such as you do on slower boats, where you steer the first half of the 'S' to get the boom across. As soon as you can feel the boom moving across and about to slam on to the new gybe, you do the second part of the 'S' to bear away the boat back on to a dead downwind or very broad reaching angle, so that the boat stays underneath the rig. In that sense, gybing an asymmetric skiff is no different to gybing any other kind of sailing boat. It's just that a lot of asymmetric boats with their fully battened and over canvassed rigs require that bit more precision. That's why making the most of your crew weight as quickly as possible is the key to surviving a difficult gybe.

Too much heel going into the gybe could make it tricky to recover from this one. . .

Nice and flat for this gybe, but get ready to bear away again the moment the boom flips across

Hoisting the Gennaker

Hoisting the gennaker is something that you should attempt for the first time only in light-to-medium airs. Hopefully you'll have already done your shore drills, so you've got some of your routines worked out between the helm and the crew. Here are some of the basic rules and responsibilities of each of the sailors during the hoist.

Most championship race courses are based on port-hand rounding, which means that you'll be bearing away from a beat onto a starboard reach or run before hoisting the gennaker.

So sail upwind normally. The helm needs to tell the crew to get ready to bear away. If any controls need easing at this stage then do so. These may be easing the cunningham and the vang

Stevie Morrison and Ben Rhodes set the gennaker on their way to winning the 49er World Championships

As soon as the kite reaches the top, Ben picks up the leeward gennaker sheet, gets the gennaker setting and joins Stevie on the trapeze. . . . *(Continued)*

Ben goes out on the trapeze handle and hands the gennaker sheet to Steve until he's got safely hooked on. Then Ben takes back the sheet and both sailors lower themselves on the wire for more righting moment . . . *(Continued)*

and, keeping the boat nice and flat, you ease the main and the jib together and bear the boat away onto quite a deep broad reach so that the crew can come in off the trapeze.

At this point, keeping the boat upright becomes the helm's responsibility, creating a level and steady platform for the crew to be able to pull the halyard and hoist the gennaker, which on many

And that's the kind of hoist that wins world championships!

boats also pulls out the bowsprit. The more stable the boat, the less the crew needs to worry about anything else and he or she can focus on hoisting the gennaker as quickly and efficiently as possible.

Once the gennaker is hoisted the crew should join the helm on the windward side gunnel (provided there's enough wind) and start the sheeting on the gennaker sheet. The helm may also need to head up at this point, to get the gennaker filling properly, so heading up from a broad reach onto a slightly tighter reach, until the sail sets. At the moment when the sail does fill, then the boat will lurch forward with the acceleration. As the apparent wind builds, the boat will lean over, so you will need either to hike it down or bear away – or most likely a combination of the two – so that you're heading lower and the boat remains upright.

OUTHAUL? LEAVE IT OUT

Once you're up and running at full speed, check that cunningham has released properly, that the vang is set, and ease outhaul if necessary. On most high-speed asymmetrics easing the outhaul makes little difference, and is just one more thing to remember to pull on at the leeward mark. So, unless you really think it's going to make a noticeable difference, leave the outhaul in its upwind position.

DAGGERBOARD

Leave the daggerboard or the centreboard down. Whatever position you have it for upwind, 99% of the time it will be just right for going downwind. The gennaker moves the centre of effort of the sail plan forwards, so you need the lateral resistance of the board for the sail plan to work against. There is one example where you might want to raise the board in light winds, as one of our experts, Dave Hivey, will explain later on.

Common mistakes

Too soon? The crew needs to make sure the boat is safely downwind before stepping into the boat to start the hoist

Bear away, no really bear away!

A common mistake with the hoist is for the helm not to have borne away enough, so that when the crew starts hoisting the kite, there's a danger of the kite filling halfway up, which then makes the job of finishing off the hoist much more difficult and also increases your chance of capsizing. So it's vital to make sure you've done a deep enough bear-away. This will help keep the gennaker in the wind shadow of the mainsail, which means that it's easier to hoist because there's less wind resistance for the crew to work against.

It is possible to bear away too much, but this doesn't happen very often, but you'll know about it when you've done it, because you'll capsize. That's the only limitation of sailing too deep. There are good tactical reasons for sailing deep at this point in a race as well, but we can come on to that later.

Picking your moment in waves

Another golden rule is that, if you're sailing in waves, make sure you pick your moment before the crew runs forward to start the hoist. Fast skiffs frequently outrun the waves – even without

Make sure a wave isn't going to give you a nasty surprise mid-hoist!

the gennaker hoisted. Timing is everything. Wait until the bow has ploughed through the back of a wave and make sure that there's going to be sufficient time to get the majority of the hoist completed before the bow goes into the back of the next wave.

Smooth systems, strong arms: the key to a fast and safe hoist

The crew's responsibility is to be able to hoist the gennaker smoothly and quickly and, if the boat is well rigged and everything is running smoothly, then a fit crew should be able to arm-over-arm hoist, i.e. their body is more or less still, they're standing up in the middle of the boat and each arm is alternating, going from being down by the halyard block to going up above the crew's head before the next arm takes over and does the same action. Sometimes, if the gennaker fills halfway up, or if it's waterlogged and heavy from a nosedive or a capsize, then 'arm-over-arming' a hoist is not going to be possible. Instead, grab the halyard with both hands and with straight arms and, most importantly, a straight back, and use your knees to do the hard work. Basically, adopt the same position as a weightlifter about to lift a heavy weight. Obviously this is a lot slower, but at times it's the only option available to you to complete the hoist. The risk is that the slower the hoist, the more vulnerable you become to the gennaker flopping into the water off the leeward side of the boat, and then trawling the gennaker. That's when the real trouble begins, but we'll save that for another chapter!

Expert Advice

Geoff Carveth, hoisting in sportsboats

First you must fully bear away before you even start hoisting. And the worst way to steer is with the rudder. Try to make it a slow turn so you're using minimal rudder. Ease loads of mainsheet with the vang eased to help spin the boat away from the wind. If you have a spacer leg from the windward mark, get everything prepared as much as possible. Ease cunningham, ease vang, ease backstay. But don't pull out the pole until you're close to bearing away. One of the SB20 class rules is that pulling out the pole has to be part of the hoisting process, so you can't have it pre-set too soon.

Reasons why the hoist can go wrong

1. Kite goes in the water: Usually this is due to pulling on the tack line too soon. Make sure the kite halyard is halfway up the mast before pulling on the tack line, otherwise you're in danger of trawling.
2. Kite gets stuck behind the main or on the jib: Don't let the boom out to the shroud, keep it sheeted in a little to give the kite a clear runway between the leeward side of the mainsail and the leeward shroud. Use the windward jib sheet to sheet, the clew of the jib into the mast. This creates a nice gap for the kite to exit from the bag, and makes it much easier to pull the tack line out.

Kite going up twisted during a SB20 hoist

3. Kite twists during the hoist: If the helm – who has already been passed the kite sheet before the bear-away – keeps the sheet loosely tensioned then the kite is less likely to twist on the way up. Don't sail too deep or the kite is more likely to wrap. On the other hand, don't sail too high or the kite will set before it's got to the top of the mast.

Dave Hivey: Hoisting in hiking boats

(Continued)

The bear-away

The crew should never ever go in for the hoist until the boat's fully borne away. With light winds it's very easy, you just bear away. When it gets breezy it becomes a little bit more critical on the timing. The crew should never go in until I say 'OK', which is just after the boat starts to bear away. Once it starts to go, that's fine. If the crew goes in too late, then it might actually capsize to windward although that doesn't happen very often. More often you see people going into the boat too soon before the bear-away has begun.

Dave Hivey and Mari Shepherd on a windy wavy day in the RS200. Safely borne away, Mari stands up to start hoisting. . . *(Continued)*

Half way through the hoist, a big wave threatens a nosedive, so Dave hikes as far aft as possible, leaving Mari free to continue hoisting. . . *(Continued)*

As Mari completes the hoist, she picks up the gennaker sheet and gets ready to join Dave on the windward gunnel.

The hoist

To do a fast hoist the crew needs to be on his or her feet, so they can hoist hand over hand without ever missing the halyard. Which means if the hoist goes wrong it's the helm's fault because he or she hasn't given the crew a stable platform. So when I bear away I'm always looking to keep the boat plumb upright all the way through the hoist.

If there are no other boats around us, I'll be looking to go as low as possible to make the platform as stable as possible. I'll drop right down and I will bring my body weight in as well. If we're going round with lots of boats, then sometimes I have to make sure that the kicker is all the way off. I don't ease the main too much to make sure that it's not powered up too much. I hike out pretty hard if I have to hold my height to make sure we stay high while the crew is doing the hoist but, again, it's really important that you keep that stable platform even when you're trying to hold height for tactical reasons.

Rick Perkins: Hoisting in singlehanded skiffs

Obviously you're fired up to get down to the leeward mark as quickly as possible, but patience is key in the hoist. If you start the hoist before the boat's properly positioned, your hoist is likely to go bad, especially if you're in a singlehanded boat. You don't have

(Continued)

the opportunity of crews jumping out on the wire whilst you're mid-manoeuvre. So the first thing is to get the boat set up for the hoist.

Make sure you're fully through the bear-away and the boat is flat and stable. At this point the mainsheet will be fully out to the stopper knot, with the boom almost touching the leeward shroud. Once you've got the boat tracking, crouching over the tiller with the tiller in the crook of your knee so you can keep the boat going in a straight line, get stuck into the halyard. There's not much friction in the Musto Skiff system, so attack the halyard and get the head of the kite up to the top as quickly as possible. Pull it up with big arm pulls, dropping the halyard you've just pulled, keeping the rope moving through your hands so you don't create a knot in the halyard.

A good tip for making sure the kite has reached the top is to have a black mark on your halyard which reaches the cleat just as you've completed the hoist. When the black mark is on the cleat you know that the kite is properly hoisted, so get the sheet on as soon as possible. If you leave the sheet flapping around whilst you get yourself steadied, there's a chance that your kite could get hourglassed, so sheet on as you get up to the windward rack. Sheet on the mainsheet, hook on and start trapezing.

Lowering the Gennaker

When you want to lower the gennaker, always give yourself more time than you think you need. You'll particularly start noticing this when you start racing against other boats and you'll find that the leeward mark often comes up quicker than you expect. You'll need even more time if you're dropping into a bag.

There's nothing worse than dropping the gennaker too late. Much better to drop it just a little bit too early and

have a bit too much time to get ready for the rounding rather than not enough. So, on a standard drop, the crew can either just drop the spinnaker sheet or, if you want to keep the speed on for a little bit longer, the crew can pass the sheet to the helm who'll hold it in his front hand, whilst the crew goes forwards to drop the gennaker.

Dropping into a chute

Standing over the halyard one foot either side, the crew releases the spinnaker halyard at the cleat and starts catching the rapidly falling gennaker by arm-over-arm dropping, pulling on

SMOOTH RUN PAST THE FORESTAY

If you find that the kite is particularly hard to get in because it's bunching up on the forestay, remember that tip for putting a spacer knot between two of the kite patches. Also, if class rules permit, you might want to put a piece of plastic tubing on the lower few feet of the forestay to give the kite a smoother run.

the retrieval line in front of the retrieval block, and behind the cleat if your boat is set up this way. The benefit of this is that you are unlikely to let the halyard re-cleat on the way down.

You'll find the drop a lot easier than the hoist, because gravity's doing a lot of the work for you so you'll find the first bit of the drop very easy and as soon as the crew starts this first piece of the drop, if the helm is still holding the sheet, they should release at this point and then, as the first retrieval patch comes round the forestay and goes into the mouth of the chute, this is when it gets harder. If you have the strength you still keep on arm-over-arming. If not, revert to the weight-lifter's stance – straight arms, straight back – and use your knees to do the last few pulls to safely get the gennaker tucked away with the head of the sail just disappearing at the end of the final pull.

Just as with the hoist, keeping the boat upright, keeping it stable, is all down to the helm. Chances are that you won't need to change direction that much during the drop, because you'll have already been sailing fairly deep anyway, but really all you're doing is looking to keep the mast dead upright, above the boat, making it as easy as possible for the crew just to focus on getting the gennaker safely stowed.

Dropping into a bag

Dropping into a bag requires good timing, otherwise there's a danger of dropping the gennaker in the water and trawling it. The helm first needs to bear away close to a dead run, taking all the apparent wind and pressure off the gennaker. The crew will then have less of a fight on

Make sure the bowman has plenty of time to get the kite bagged before the leeward rounding. The price for dropping too late is much greater than dropping too early. . .

their hands to get the sail into the bag. First release the tack line and gather most of the foot and start stuffing it into the bag. Release the kite halyard and arm-over-arm the kite into the bag as quickly as possible. If you have a retractable bowsprit, make sure the bowsprit slides back into the boat to minimise the chance of hitting any other boats during a congested mark rounding.

What if you have overstood the layline for the leeward mark and don't have the space to bear away on to a dead run? On smaller asymmetrics it's still possible to get the kite down on the windward side, but you need to be fast. While the helm (or another crew member) still has the kite sheeted on, the forward crew person grabs the lazy windward sheet. Then the crew releases the halyard and tack line in quick succession and the kite will fall very quickly towards the water. But, if you're fast, the crew can haul in on the windward kite sheet and, provided you get the clew of the gennaker past the forestay and on to the foredeck, you're pretty much safe from there. Just keep on hauling the kite in around the forestay and stuffing it in the bag as you go. It's not pretty, it feels risky, but it's easier than it sounds. If you've got fast arms you won't have a problem.

In lighter winds, the bowman can sit to leeward and complete the rest of the gennaker tidying as the boat goes upwind. . .

Expert Tips

Geoff Carveth: Dropping kites on sportsboats

The ideal kite drop means that you are set up for a standard hoist out of the leeward side of the bag at the next windward mark. So, on a port-rounding course, you're looking to drop the kite on the port side of the boat.

This Melges 24 crew pay a high price for getting the gennaker down late. Now they're really slow as they turn upwind for the next beat...

The easiest way is to do a gybe-drop, with the crew keeping the kite on the port side as the boat gybes. Release the pole and tackline first, and gather the foot of the sail in before releasing the halyard, at which point you drop the kite into the bag.

A leeward take-down is not as easy, but not too difficult either. The helmsman just needs to keep the boat well borne away to take the pressure out of the gennaker and get it into the lee of the mainsail and jib where it's easier to handle and get into the bag.

Start dropping the kite earlier than you think. The extra distance you gain from a late drop is more than offset by the struggle you'll have trying to fight the kite into the bag once you turn up into the breeze. And helmsmen – leave it to the crew to decide when to bag the kite. They know how long it takes, better than you, so don't make it harder for them than it already is.

Rick Perkins: Dropping kites in skiffs

If you're late starting your drop, you'll be sailing past the mark on a run, whilst your competitors are sailing upwind in the opposite direction on a beat. Overshooting the leeward mark because you've started your drop too late is a disaster. Not only have you gone too far, you're giving away ground as you sail away from the buoy. You've then got to recover that ground by sailing back upwind slowly, relative to the speed at which you went down the run. So my mantra is: 'if in doubt, get it down early'. One of the ways I practise this is in training: I will sail past the buoy and, when I go past the buoy I start the

Andy has borne away and stays in the back footloop to keep the bow out while Mari works on getting the kite back into the chute... *(Continued)*

Note how far back Mari is standing, helping Andy keep the bow out. If she had to get this into a bag, a nosedive would be a greater risk than it is here...
(Continued)

With the kite safely back in the chute, Mari joins Andy on the trapeze, ready to put maximum righting moment on the windward rack before Andy rounds up for the beat.

drop, finish the drop, harden up and then look back and see how far away the buoy is. It's amazing how far you've travelled during that drop. If you do that exercise quite frequently and maybe once prior to the start of each race, you'll get a better feel for the distance that it takes to drop the kite so you're better equipped to judge when to start the drop.

Once the drop is started, my normal process is that I'll ease the mainsheet out to the shroud as I come in off the wire. Then, oversheet the kite so it's tucked behind the mainsail, uncleat the halyard and then use big explosive pulls on the downhaul to get it into the sock. It's amazing that the kite seems quite well behaved behind the mainsail. So, even if you're a bit slow getting it down, it doesn't seem to fall into the water and end up trawling in the Musto Skiff. I've found that to be more of a problem in other classes. I'm guessing it must be the design of the sock mouth or the position of the pole or whatever it is.

Here's the process again: main out on the shroud, oversheet the foot, uncleat the halyard, bag it up quick. Then you have got time to get the downhaul and the vang on, hook on and then sheet in around the buoy.

(Continued)

Musto Skiff sailor has got his kite bagged nice and early, leaving him clear for a controlled mark rounding

Dave Hivey: Dropping kites in hiking dinghies

As you approach the leeward mark, make sure you're coming in a little bit high, giving yourself the ability to bear away before you go for the drop. You don't want to be too powered up as the crew goes in for the drop, because it makes the boat quite difficult

As with the hoist, Mari stands up to speed up the drop. . . .
(Continued)

and Mari completes the drop as Dave rounds the leeward mark.

to keep stable at that point. If you can come in just slightly above the layline it gives you the option to bear away and take the power out of the sails. There's nothing wrong with doing bit of a bear-away and coming back up to the mark again as long as you are really careful about not opening your transom to other boats looking to get room on you at the mark. But. as with the hoist, it's vital to give the crew that nice stable platform.

As you're about to drop the kite, there are two things you can do; either the crew passes the kite sheet back to the helm, or the crew can stand on the sheet so they keep the kite filled that fraction longer. It also means that the kite is not allowed to flap, so it is far less likely to be twisted for the next hoist. And it also keeps the sheet taut, discouraging it from looping around the bow and possibly falling over the front and getting stuck underneath the boat, which can happen on the RS200 and 400.

Dropping the gennaker on multihulls

World Champions Darren Bundock and Glenn Ashby show how it's done on a windy day in the Tornado

Glenn comes in to haul the kite back into the chute while Darren starts to steer up for the rounding

Rounding up this soon doesn't exactly make it easy for the crew, and leaves little margin for error. So don't attempt this straight away. Start the drop earlier and give yourself time to prepare for the rounding. These pictures give you something to aspire to when you feel you're ready to take it up a notch . . . *(Continued)*

Glenn must be puffing hard, but there's no time to take a breather as Darren luffs up around the leeward mark

That's how it's done by the best. Darren and Glenn are straight back into upwind mode.

Gybing with the Gennaker

The rules for a successful gybe are very simple: keep it fast and keep it flat. Let's look at the components of a good asymmetric gybe.

Not too much rudder!

Gybing the gennaker is very different to gybing on a single-sailed boat or even on a boat with a conventional spinnaker. What takes most people by surprise is how little the boat needs to be turned to get through the gybe, particularly when you're travelling at speed. One of the big mistakes for newcomers to asymmetrics is for the helm to use far too much rudder and to make too much of a handbrake turn through the gybe. In medium to strong airs too much rudder can result in you capsizing. Using small amounts of rudder has a big effect compared with gybing other kinds of boat.

Keep it flat

The other difference from conventional dinghies is that it's much more important to keep the boat flat throughout the manoeuvre. There's little need for roll gybing, except in the very lightest of breezes. If you attempt a roll gybe in anything stronger, again you're probably going to end up capsizing. You won't go too far wrong if you can keep the boat flat all the way through the manoeuvre.

Your first asymmetric gybe

First I'm going to assume that you've already done some dry-land practising, working through your footwork, body movement and hand movements, and that, as helm and crew, you've made a plan as to how you're going to gybe.

Andy Budgen and Mari Shepherd hadn't sailed the Rebel Skiff before, so this isn't a bad first effort for a gybe. As they come off the trapeze, Mari keeps the kite filling for maximum speed into the gybe, and note how little the tiller moves from the centreline. . . *(Continued)*

A bit of windward heel creeps in, and it would have been better to keep the boat flat or even slightly heeled to leeward. Also, the kite is starting to billow out the front and would have been better if Mari could hold on to the old kite sheet for longer... *(Continued)*

Andy eases the boom to the shroud to keep the boat on its feet, but at least they're safely through the gybe with a flat boat. He swaps steering hands as Mari hauls on the new kite sheet. . . . *(Continued)*

With the kite filling on the new gybe and the boat accelerating, Andy and Mari hook up on the trapeze and get moving to full pace again....

Also, don't give yourself the challenge of learning to gybe in a Force Five! Choose a light-to-medium breeze when you try things out for the first time.

So, here goes. As you're approaching the gybe the helm needs to make sure that there's space behind and to leeward before you begin changing course. You must make sure there are no other boats in your way and that you have a clear space to gybe into, because the direction changes are so much greater compared with conventional kinds of boat when they gybe.

Once you know that you've got space to gybe, tell the crew to get ready to gybe. If they're on the trapeze (hang on, what are they doing on trapeze? This is your first gybe! One thing at a time, please), this might mean that they come in off the trapeze first so that they're in a position to move through the boat as the gybe begins.

As the boat bears away, move your body weight to the centre line, keeping the boat flat so that, as the power in the rig decreases, so too does your righting moment. As the boom gybes across the middle of the boat, you should have reached the middle of the boat, with your head below boom height!

As the boat exits the gybe and gets on to its new course, crew weight should move smoothly and quickly to the new windward side of the cockpit, about the same time as you expect the boom to complete its arc and for the mainsail to start setting on the new side.

In full-power conditions, where you're using maximum righting movement downwind, the ideal gybe is one where you spend the absolute minimum time in the middle of the boat. You want to be full hiking (or trapezing) on one gybe and into full hiking on the new gybe with as little downtime as possible. Not only is this fast, it's safer too. Lightweight asymmetric dinghies are like bicycles. Both are hard to keep upright when they're stopped or travelling slowly.

Two types of gybe: 'blow-through' or 'pull-through'?

There are two ways the crew can manage the gennaker through the gybe. Here we'll call the two versions the 'blow-through' gybe and the 'pull-through' gybe.

Blow!

The blow-through involves holding on to the old sheet through the gybe and keeping the gennaker sheeted in its old position until the wind on the new windward side of the boat is blowing the kite against the jib and forestay. At this point the crew releases the old sheet and rapidly sheets on with the new gennaker sheet. If you do it quick enough, you can snap on the new sheet and the kite will fill instantly on the new gybe.

This works particularly well on boats with long bowsprits such as the International 14, where the kite has a nice big space to blow past the forestay. It works less well on boats like the 49er

Mari applying the blow-through technique in the RS200. For most conditions, this is the simplest and most trouble-free technique...

with a short bowsprit, making the gennaker prone to sticking against the jib, particularly if the kite is wet and old. Newer kites with their slippery finish tend to blow through much more nicely than older ones.

Pull!

The pull-through gybe involves the crew starting to haul on the new sheet as you begin the gybe manoeuvre. As the boom is gybing, the clew of the kite should be coming past the forestay and, by the time you're onto the new course for the new gybe, the kite should be in place and already setting on the new side.

When you get the timing right, the pull-through gybe is very fast and efficient, requiring less steering to get the flow reattached on the gennaker. But it requires more physical effort and more timing to get it right.

In light winds the pull-through technique is the more reliable option. On this Melges 24, you can see the bowman helping the trimmer pull the gennaker round on to the new side even before the mainsail has gybed. *(Continued)*

Even if you don't have the luxury of a bowman up on your foredeck, this technique works a treat on most kinds of asymmetric dinghies and catamarans...

Which?

So, which is best? In the majority of cases, the blow-through gybe will serve you very well. It requires less effort and less timing to get it right, but if you find the kite is sticking to the jib, it might mean it's time to shell out some money on a new one. You should still practise the pull-through gybe too, though. It is the best light-wind option, as we'll explain in the next chapter.

Timing your move

Whilst you're learning the timing of all of this, there's even something to be said for getting to the new side a little bit sooner than you think you need. Better to get there too early than too late. The mistake that many people make is to get there too late, resulting in the boat gybing (a good thing) but capsizing almost immediately afterwards (a bad thing).

On the other hand, if you go through the boat too early, this can mean that the boat slows up too quickly and you never end up actually completing the gybe. The boom will never actually cross the centre line, which means that you might broach and capsize to leeward on the old

Dave and Mari at full pace as they prepare to gybe the RS200. . . *(Continued)*

Dave and Mari keep the boat nice and flat through the gybe. At one point it looks like a bit of windward heel is going to creep in, but.... *(Continued)*

they swiftly correct with a combination of steering and bodyweight faster up to the new side of the boat... *(Continued)*

Dave has been steering with his hands behind his back, and finally swaps hands for the new gybe.

gybe. This error tends to be the less frequent of the two so, if in doubt about your timing, move your weight over to the new side sooner than you think you need to.

You'll soon gain in experience and confidence, and feel ready to start gybing faster. In planing conditions you can even gybe with the boat slightly heeled to leeward all the way through the manoeuvre. If you think about it, that's exactly what a windsurfer does when he's powering through a carve gybe. The mast is always pointing away from the sailor (to leeward) and it's almost as though the tip of the mast is fixed in space, with the board rotating around the tip of the mast. Fast asymmetric dinghies respond to the same treatment.

THE POWER OF THE BATTENS

Andy catches the boom before it slams across. This takes the 'oomph' out of the sail and reduces the slamming moment that would occur if he just let the boom fly across unchecked. When the battens in the mainsail flick to the new side, it creates a power surge just when you don't want it - at least not in heavy winds. Andy's controlled release of the boom minimises the slamming force. . .

For sailors used to sailing conventional dinghies with soft sails, the surge of power created by an asymmetric dinghy can come as a shock. Part of the reason for this is that most modern asymmetric boats are equipped with powerful, fully-battened mainsails. When these stiff battens flick at the end of the gybe, they create a power surge that needs to be counteracted, and that's why there's an added incentive - compared with older more traditional boats - to get your weight onto the new side a little bit quicker. If you leave it too late, the power of the 'batten flick' can result in you capsizing, but if you get your timing right, you can harness the 'batten flick' to help accelerate you up to full speed on the new gybe.

THE MEASURE OF A GOOD GYBE

We've already stressed the importance of travelling as fast as possible through the whole gybing manoeuvre. You know you're gybing really well when the boom seems to float from one side to the other through the manoeuvre. In strong winds this is one of the sweetest differences between gybing a conventional boat – where the boom nearly always slams from one side to the other – and a fast asymmetric. Even if the wind is blowing 18 knots, if you're gybing with 12 knots' boatspeed, there's only 6 knots of force moving the boom across. This is a great way of gauging your progress with gybing. The more the boom 'floats', the better you're gybing.

Summary

This 49er crew have given themselves a lot to do. Either the helm turned the boat too fast or the crew was too slow moving to the new side and needs to get himself out on the trapeze before the kite sets and powers up.

Remember the two 'F' words: Flat and Fast.

The speed that you turn the boat needs to be matched by the speed you move through the boat. If you can't move that fast, don't turn so fast!

If you're managing to gybe but capsizing immediately afterwards, chances are you turned the boat too quickly or didn't move through to the new side of the boat quick enough. Either slow down the rate of turn and/or move through the boat more quickly.

If you capsize before even completing the gybe, chances are you've slowed down too much and the pressure in the mainsail has become too much to handle. Remember that asymmetric dinghies are like bicycles – unstable at low speed. So, first make sure you're travelling as close to maximum speed before beginning your gybe. If that by itself doesn't solve the problem, try increasing the rate of turn with the rudder and keep your crew weight hiking out as long as possible before starting the gybing manoeuvre.

Expert Tips

Geoff Carveth: Gybing in sportsboats

Going into the gybe with maximum speed is vital in strong winds

(Continued)

Gybing: Drag it or back it?

You've got two choices about how to gybe the gennaker, and this applies to many asymmetric boats, not just the SB20.

Back it!   This is the best choice for any conditions over 6 knots of breeze. As the helm steers into the gybe, the sheet-hand keeps the kite sheeted or even pulls on some more sheet so that as the boat gybes the kite is laying against the new windward side of the jib. At this point, release the old sheet and sheet in the new kite sheet as quickly as possible. If you get it right, you'll have the new sheet snapped on and the kite instantly filling on the new gybe, launching the boat back up to speed again.

The pull-through   Backing the kite doesn't work well below 6 knots and, if your kite is old and wet, then there's a danger of it sticking to the jib like porridge to a blanket. Times like these call for the 'pull-through'. This time the sheet-hand releases the old kite sheet and starts hauling on the new kite sheet as the helm initiates the gybe. Again, if you're fast and smooth enough, you should be able to have the kite set by the time you're on the new course for the new gybe.

Rick Perkins: Gybing singlehanded skiffs

Gybing a singlehander, the mainsail needs to stay cleated in a 'safe' position while the helm focuses on steering and gybing the gennaker. . .

Ideally you need three or four hands to gybe an asymmetric singlehanded trapeze boat like the Musto Skiff. But, assuming you don't, the key is to develop and learn a process that you then go out and try to implement. If you kind of try and make it up as you go along as you're bouncing down the water at high speed, it's very hard to work out what to do next unless you have a clear plan in the first place.

If you learn what you're trying to achieve through shore drills, through studying videos on YouTube or through photo sequences, you've got a much better chance of actually executing a good gybe than if you are just making it up as you go along. So have a clear set of processes and practise them in your head and on shore before trying it on the water.

It's vital to keep the speed on as you approach the gybe. It's very easy to come in off the wire and sit around and start fiddling around with your bits of string. While you're doing this the boat is slowing and the rig is loading. OK, so once I've made the decision to gybe I'm taking the slack out of the windward kite sheet and, depending on the wind conditions, I might ease the main slightly. Not a lot, just a little bit such that it's not quite so pinned in once I've got through to the new gybe. So, as you're about to start turning into the gybe, take the slack out of the windward kite sheet, trim the mainsail out if needed, come in off the wire, bear away gently and cross the boat early – possibly even before the boom has gybed. If you watch

Musto Skiff World Champion Richard Stenhouse uses the 'superman punch' to pull the kite around the forestay and through to the new gybe

(Continued)

Dave and Mari let the boat heel to windward a little too much for these windy conditions, but. . . *(Continued)*

good control of the rudder and the mainsail on the exit means they get away
with it. A flatter boat with less roll would have been better. . . *(Continued)*

Back on an even keel and going fast again.

a video of a good sailor gybing in slow motion, you'll see that they are stepping through the boat on the inside of the turn, getting on the new side before the boom has crossed. As soon as the boom comes across give the new kite sheet an enormous pull, what is known in the Musto Skiff fleet as the 'Superman punch'. So you're picking up the new sheet from the windward ratchet block and pulling it across your body in one big long pull to try to get the spinnaker around on to the new side as quickly as possible. Sit down on the new wing so you've got a bit of weight on the new side with the boat still going fast. If you get the Superman punch right, hopefully the kite is filled on the new side. If not, sheet in until the kite fills, settle down, hook on, out you go on the wire, and sheet the mainsail back in for maximum boatspeed.

Dave Hivey: Gybing hiking dinghies

The helm should be the one to initiate the gybe, as they're the one doing the tactics and making the decisions downwind. I'll try to give the crew warning if possible. Sometimes, if a boat around us gybes, I'll literally just have to say, 'We're going'. But let's say we've got an ideal situation where we're going to pick a spot on a wave. I'll ask, 'Are you ready to go?' The crew will basically say, 'Yes!' or 'No'. If it's a 'Yes!', I start to initiate the gybe as the crew starts to go in. As the crew starts to go forward I will then lean out and start to initiate the gybe to make sure it's got some windward heel on the way in, which will start with an ease of the mainsail. I then go for my gybing strap (a grab rope hanging from the centre of the boom) and pull it across nice and early – a lot earlier than you'd think. As I gybe I'll pull the gybing strap across and then hold it in the middle for a second just to make sure it doesn't slam out onto the far side, and then slowly ease it out as I cross the other side with my body. The key move next is to bring the boat up onto the breeze on the new gybe depending on where the crew is. If the crew spent too long in the front because he or she didn't get the kite sheet, fell over, or anything that might have happened in the gybe, then you need to hold the boat in that stable downwind phase for a bit longer before you come up. If you see the crew hit the new side with the kite sheet then we can start to heat it up a lot more. I'll vary the speed of the gybe depending on where the crew is, and that makes the gybing an awful lot safer. The crew keeps the old sheet where it is, sometimes even snapping it on a little during the gybe. Then, when the kite backs against the jib, the crew releases the old sheet with one hand and, with the other, snaps on the new sheet as the kite blows through to the new gybe. When you get your timing right, there's very little effort involved and the kite fills instantly, making it safe and fast.

'PRE-GYBING THE MAINSAIL'

I like to pull the boom across using the boom strap. If you wait for the boom to cross in its own time, when it does gybe, you'll never beat it to the new side. If you wait for the wind to catch the new side of the mainsail and blow the boom across, it will just slam across to the new side. You'll have no chance of matching that power surge with your body weight on the other side when it hits the new side. If you pull it across slightly earlier than that point, you'll find that there's almost no power in it when you pull it across. You can

Note the extra line hanging off the centre of the boom next to the mainsheet. This is the boom strap, which Dave grabs to force the boom over early during a gybe. . .

just slowly pull it over your head and then ease it out on the new side, and there'd be no power at all. And remember to slow the boom down as it runs out to the new leeward shroud. When it's windy, I'll oversheet the main a little bit because that reduces the power in the mainsail (because you're presenting less sail area to the wind). If you were to pull the boom across and just throw it across, you'll get a 'snap' when it hits the new side. That will be quite hard to steer to and match the body weight to. I want a nice, smooth gybe the whole way through. So what I do is, as the wind catches the boom on the new gybe, hold the boom for a brief moment and slowly ease the main out to the shroud - this will get rid of the snap effect.

Gybing in Light Airs

Gybing asymmetrics in light airs is one of those things that's not difficult to do, but it's difficult to do well. Gybing from one gybe to the other takes time for the disturbed wind to reattach on the new side of the sails, and it requires deft movement to keep the boat moving smoothly through the manoeuvre.

While a good general rule in asymmetric sailing is a 'flat boat at all times', here a bit of windward roll in the gybe will help keep the speed on through the manoeuvre and will give you the opportunity to pull the boat upright on the new gybe as you accelerate on to your new course.

In conditions where there's not sufficient wind to blow the kite past the forestay for the standard 'blow-through' gybe, now is the time to bring the 'pull-through' gybe into play. Because the wind is light and the boat is moving slowly, this is a fairly simple manoeuvre to execute.

Once you've gybed, sail high onto a reach to build the apparent wind on the new heading. As the boat accelerates and the power comes on again, you can then steer back to your normal heading. Look up and

The exception that breaks the golden rule of 'Flat and Fast'. This Swedish 49er applies heel and roll to their gybe in light winds, to help the battens flick over and to be able to accelerate the boat out of the gybe with crew weight. Any windier than a Force 2, though, and all you want to do is gybe flat. . .

make sure that the mainsail battens have flicked through to the new gybe, which brings us on to our next section. . .

Gybing a fully-battened mainsail in light airs

Fully battened mainsails put more power in the rig, which is great when you're going in a straight line. But fully-battened mainsails also make life more challenging through the manoeuvres, particularly through the gybe.

In light-to-medium conditions it can be difficult to convince all the battens to flick on to the new gybe when you are coming out of the manoeuvre. In fact, sometimes you can see people sailing along for hundreds of yards with the battens inverted because they haven't looked up and realised that the sail has refused to set properly by itself. There are times when it needs a helping hand. So, after a light wind gybe, make sure that you do look up and check the set of the sail.

In a boat with two people or less, this is the helm's job. In a boat where you have a full-time mainsheet-hand then it's the mainsheet-hand's job to check that these battens are behaving themselves. Quite often it's the top one or two battens that have failed to gybe. It might be that you can give the mainsail a couple of vigorous pumps to convince the battens to flick over, but make sure that you're staying within the rules when you do this. You don't want to be given a penalty by an umpire for looking like you're pumping the sail beyond the bounds of the dreaded Rule 42.

Gybing the battens on a fully-battened mainsail is one of the challenges of light airs. . .

If a couple of vigorous pumps doesn't have the desired effect, then try tensioning the vang and even the cunningham. With the big square-headed mainsails that are in vogue with the really high-performance asymmetrics these days, such as the 18-foot Skiff and the International 14, the battens can be particularly stubborn. Gybing the International 14, for instance, it almost becomes part of the routine out of the gybe for the crew to reach forward, pull on an armful of cunningham until you can hear the batten pop and then release the cunningham again to get maximum power back into the mainsail. If you're doing a lot of gybing and the batten consistently refuses to pop through any gybe, it might even be worth leaving the cunningham on all the way down the run. What you lose in straight-line speed will be minimal compared with the time that you save from not faffing around trying to gybe that stubborn batten all the time.

In very light winds you will probably have to make sure that all the battens are gybed, because the force of the wind won't do any of the work for you. In these conditions, whoever in the boat is controlling the mainsail downwind has the responsibility of giving the boom a flick as the boat goes through the gybe. On many boats the best way to do this is to grab the boom directly, or by one of the mainsheet blocks hanging off the boom, and use that as a solid hand-hold to give the boom a vigorous shake just as you're gybing onto the new course.

In a singlehanded boat like the Musto Skiff, this is really difficult because you're trying to gybe and set the kite through the manoeuvre and also make sure that the battens have popped. If you're struggling to do all these things at once, then make flicking the battens your top priority because it's much easier to do it smoothly, or at least do it during the course of the manoeuvre and then get the kite set later. It's much worse to come out of a gybe, get settled, and then look up and find that you've still got to shake those mainsail battens through. You'll then have to upset the balance and the trim of the boat to get that job done so you're really having to do everything twice. Give the battens your highest priority in light winds. Get them sorted and once the battens are through, then you can get on with all your other jobs.

CHAPTER 3

ADVANCED MOVES

S o far you've equipped yourself with the basic moves for getting you safely around a course. Now let's look at some of the more advanced moves and add a few more weapons to your armoury. One of the most daring moves is the gybe set. Let's start there.

Gybe Set

On most championship courses the course is set for port roundings at the windward mark. The easiest and most straight forward hoist is a straight set on starboard gybe. But the ability to gybe-set is an important addition to your tactical armoury. On a typical port-rounding course this sees you bearing away from close-hauled starboard tack onto starboard gybe, hoisting the gennaker, gybing onto port and filling the kite all in one smooth manoeuvre. You're sailing the boat through a tight arc of about 180 degrees, perhaps more.

Sound tricky? Well, it's not a beginner's move, but a great one to be able to use during a race. If you're rounding mid-fleet with lots of boats around you, most boats will be doing a straight set on starboard gybe, so the gybe-set has the potential to get you out into clear air very quickly.

Practise first

This is certainly not one to try first time out sailing, and it's certainly not one to try in strong winds. You want to practise this manoeuvre in light-to-medium airs.

The first thing to do is to get comfortable sailing from upwind, bearing away through a smooth arc and gybing the boat onto a port gybe. It's best to practise this first without hoisting the gennaker. Only bring the gennaker into play when you've got this manoeuvre down smoothly without it. Apart from in very light winds, you want to keep the boat upright all the way through the manoeuvre.

Then, when you're comfortable doing it without the gennaker, try bringing the hoist into the process too. Initially, make sure you complete the full gybe and only start hoisting the gennaker when the boat is fully settled on port gybe.

At this point, it's the helm's responsibility to keep the boat upright while the crew stands up or does whatever is required to get in position to hoist the gennaker. On boats with the chute mouth located on the left hand side of the foredeck, to one side of the jib, the hoist actually tends to be incredibly easy because the kite is unimpeded by the jib so it tends to be quite an easy few pulls getting the kite to the top of the mast.

This 49er just about gets away with the gybe, but when you're practising, build it up step by step

However, it becomes even easier if the helmsman keeps the boat well borne away on a broad reach, possibly even a run. Applying a small amount of windward heel, say five degrees, means the kite is less likely to get tangled up with spreaders and rigging, creating a smoother passage up to the top of the mast.

One risk of hoisting the gennaker from this side of the boat, especially if you're not borne away on a dead run, is for the spinnaker to get stuck in the foretriangle, the space between the forestay and the mast. A great tip for helping avoid this is to have the jib sheeted on hard. Now, you only sheet the jib on hard when you've safely completed the whole gybing manoeuvre and you're travelling downwind, upright and in control. At that point if you pull the jib on hard, it will have no effect on the steering or stability of the boat. But what it will do is create a hard wall that will prevent the gennaker from getting stuck, giving the kite no choice but to blow out in front of the forestay. At this point the crew can snap on the gennaker sheet and get the kite filling nicely on port gybe. When the boat is up and running the crew can also ease the jib back to its normal downwind position.

Speeding it up

So that was the basic gybe-set. As you get more confident with the manoeuvre, you can speed up all the different phases of the process. The ultimate gybe-set is one where you start hoisting the gennaker, even as the boat is bearing away ready to gybe. The head of the kite hits the top of the mast, just as the boat is completing its gybe. The crew is already snapping on the new kite

sheet whilst simultaneously hooking on to the port trapeze ring, and pushing out off the side of the boat in unison with the helmsman as they catch the gennaker – just at the moment that the sail is filling and powering up.

This is an incredibly powerful manoeuvre and can accelerate the boat very quickly up to full speed on port gybe, enabling you to roll any other boats that have completed their gybe-set less effectively, as well as putting good distance between you and the boats that continued on starboard gybe on a straight set. However, you do need to be ready to apply full righting moment to the new windward side of the boat as you exit out of the gybe – if you're going to be able to control the power of the gennaker as it snaps into action. When you get this right, the acceleration is incredible, and it's one of the most rewarding manoeuvres you can do in an asymmetric boat.

Gybe Drop

The gybe-drop involves gybing and immediately dropping the gennaker all in one smooth manoeuvre. It's particularly useful for approaching a leeward mark from to leeward of other boats, and claiming inside mark rounding rights.

As with all manoeuvres involving hoisting or dropping the gennaker, it's vital the helm provides a stable and upright platform so that the crew can get on with stowing the gennaker as quickly as possible without interruption.

Gybe-dropping into a chute

In terms of boathandling, the gybe-drop requires more balance and timing than a straight drop. The key is to go into the gybe at full speed, just as you would on a normal gybe. The difference comes once you've gybed, at which point the helm needs to keep the boat borne away close to a dead run, as the crew will be aiming to get the kite down and in the chute as soon as the gybe is complete. If the crew keeps the old kite sheet tensioned as you go into the gybe, this will keep the three corners of the sail nicely separated and will encourage the kite to go into the chute untwisted, ready for a clean hoist next time.

Provided you're not in a tight battle with another boat for rounding rights, start the gybe drop nice and early in time for a clean mark rounding. . . *(Continued)*

Mari straps the kite sheet in hard, ensuring the kite is ready to drop on to the fore-deck, not in the water. . . *(Continued)*

With the boat slowing down, Dave eases the boom out to the shroud, keeping the boat flat while Mari gets into position for the drop. . . *(Continued)*

Mari stands up so she has a longer pull for arm-over-arm dropping as she retrieves the gennaker into the chute. . . *(Continued)*

Dave has steered in a wide arc, allowing him to round up close to the buoy as Mari finishes the drop and gets into full hiking mode once more. . .

Gybe-dropping into a bag

On a sportsboat like a Melges 24 or SB20, or a dinghy like a B14 or 18-foot Skiff, gybe-dropping from starboard gybe onto port ensures you'll be correctly set up for a leeward hoist at the next windward mark. So the gybe-drop is even more important for boats with gennaker bags. Also, as we discussed in the previous chapter, the straight drop into a bag is not a particularly easy manoeuvre, not compared with the simplicity of dropping into a chute. So you might as well get used to the gybe-drop as one of your standard manoeuvres.

The approach and initial phase is the same as a standard gybe. But, again, once the gybe is complete, don't steer up but keep the boat tracking downwind on, or near, a dead run. This takes all the apparent wind out of the kite and makes it easier for the crew to bag.

And again, like the gybe-drop into a chute, if the crew keeps the kite sheeted in with the old gennaker sheet as they gybe, the kite is sitting there next to you, ready to grab and easy to reach for the take down. Release the tack line first, getting the tack of the sail safely back on to the foredeck where it can't fall in the water, then release the halyard and stuff the sail into the bag as gravity gives you a helping hand. Once the kite is stowed, make sure the bowsprit is retracted back into the boat.

Better to drop too soon than too late!

Beam Reaching

Beam reaching is one of the first things that we learn to do in sailing, because it's one of the easiest things to do. In fast, lightweight skiffs and multihulls, the opposite is true. Because they are so quick to accelerate and build on their own apparent wind, they become too efficient for their own good.

In moderate-to-strong winds, sailing directly on a beam reach from one mark to another becomes impossible. As the boat accelerates and the apparent wind builds, the power rapidly increases and exceeds the righting moment available. Either you capsize, or you change direction. You either need to sail below the rhumb line, or above it, or a combination of the two. So, to stay upright and in control, you actually end up sailing a zigzag course to the mark. In skiff world, the no-go zone is known as the 'death zone'.

Spend as little time as possible in the 'Death Zone'

At any point during the reach, everyone on board needs to understand whether the helm is sailing in a high mode or a low mode. Keep a constant look-out over your windward shoulder for the next gust. If you're in high mode, get ready to luff up and ease main and jib together. If you're sailing a dinghy or skiff, make sure the boat is slightly heeled to windward before the gust hits. Once you're in the gust, get settled on the new course and look out for the next change in wind speed, whether it's a gust or a lull.

If you're sailing in low mode, again you need to keep a weather eye out for the next gust, but this time as the gust hits you bear away and ease sails to keep the boat on its feet. Once you have accelerated with the gust, head up as close to the direction of the mark as the power will allow. Sheet the sails to keep the boat flat. Generally, a reach requires massive amounts of mainsheet to move in and out, and boats where the crew plays the mainsheet are at a massive advantage because they have two arms to devote to the task. Helms who play the mainsheet are more restricted in how much sheet they can move, so steering becomes even more critical.

Beam reaching in a boat like this Devoti D-1 is simple enough, but requires more respect in a high-powered skiff

Whether you are in high or low mode, it is all about sailing as close to the death zone as you can without becoming overpowered. Sailing down a beam reach is one of the most challenging things you can do in a high-performance boat. But it's great fun when you master the technique.

Boat set-up

Sailing down a beam reach is mostly about courage and good technique, but good boat set-up will also make things easier. Do anything you can to depower the boat. This can include any or all of the following:

- pull up daggerboard
- maximum cunningham
- maximum outhaul
- minimum vang
- jib out on widest traveller car setting (if you have a track for a self-tacking jib for example), and
- mainsail traveller fully to leeward.

Remember, once you're already on the tight reach, it will be much harder or impossible to make these adjustments, so try to anticipate and alter the boat set-up before you get to that point.

Expert Advice

Charlie Ogletree, Tornado Olympic silver medallist crew: Two-sail reaching in high-performance multihulls

The traveller stays centred at all times, the downhaul stays on tight for strong winds, comes off a couple of notches for medium airs, or is released completely for the light. Easing outhaul we don't worry about, as a flat sail is good. The jib is one of the more overlooked items, but actually one of the most critical. Keep a hand on the jib sheet, whichever of you is not playing the main, so that you can adjust the jib when necessary. You should aim to have the bottom two tell-tails streaming and the top one lifting.

(Continued)

If it's going to be a long reach and is going to require a lot of mainsheet trim, I'll keep the mainsheet and the helm will focus on steering. On short reaches such as the offset leg on a windward/leeward course, I'll just play the jib and the helm will play the main.

As for the centreboards, we leave them both all the way down, as the boat needs all the foil it can get. If you're doing a long reach on a beach cat, however, pull the windward one up. If it's blowing over 20 knots, it's sometimes good to pull the leeward one up halfway, which allows the boat to side slip. In these conditions you might even want to let the traveller down a bit; the windier it gets the further down it goes.

Tight Reaching

Recent years have seen sailing become more and more focused on windward/leeward courses, with sailors becoming very specialised in the techniques of beating and running. This is particularly true in asymmetric racing where the only kind of courses are windward/leeward.

Pushing it high in an 18 footer

There are some classes like the International 14 which have always included reaches in their championship courses and continue to do so today. Also, many of us race around the cans in club racing in handicap fleets, and the ability to reach with an asymmetric sail becomes a vital skill.

Even if you only ever race on windward/leeward courses, I strongly advise you to practise your tight reaching skills. You only need to over stand a layline by a small amount, or to be on your layline when suddenly the wind increases by 5 knots, when you now find yourself well below the layline.

De-tune the boat

Early on in this book, we established that, in planing conditions, the higher you point the more apparent wind you create, and the deeper and faster you end up sailing. All these things are great when you are trying to make maximum ground downwind. But all these wonderful efficiencies are now working against you as you try to make maximum ground to windward with the kite up.

Nothing like the pressure of a rocky shore to hone your tight-reaching skills!

You will actually make better ground to windward if you can slow the boat down and get rid of some of that apparent wind. Here are some things you can do to help slow the boat and gain height:

- pull on cunningham
- ease vang
- ease jib sheet
- ease mainsheet
- daggerboard up
- let the boat heel over to leeward
- ease the kite to maximum curl before it flogs, or
- oversheet the kite!

Oversheeting the kite feels like absolutely the wrong thing to do, but I've tried it a few times in different classes and it works surprisingly well for slowing the boat down and gaining height to windward. Another extreme option I learned when crewing for Will Henderson (multiple champion in the International 14) was to jump up and down on the gunnel whilst we were twin-trapezing in the 14. Will's theory was that if smooth is fast, then rough is slow! If it reduces the efficiency of the boat, then it might well work. We didn't do it often enough to prove it one

An International 14 pushing for height, the crew curling the gennaker as much as possible

way or the other. But the overriding message here is to think of ways that you can make the boat less efficient! The more you can reduce the apparent wind, the higher you will point.

Expert Advice

Darren Bundock: High performance multihulls

Oversheeting the gennaker can help when you're trying to push for a mark you can't quite make. You can also drop the traveller down and keep mainsheet tension on, because it's working like a backstay for you. The mainsheet tension will stop the top of the mast falling off so you can drop the traveller down, which will depower the boat and let you go higher. Also, oversheeting the spinnaker takes some of that power out of the sail and let's you go high as well. And by this stage you should definitely be double trapezing.

You want to pull on cunningham, to help flatten the mainsail and twist off the top. But you've got to be a little bit careful if you have too much main cunningham on because it is bending the mast in its weakest direction, where it could break if you overstress it.

Ease jib sheet so that the jib is only slightly pulling. You could almost have it uncleated, but we have just a small amount of tension in the jib on a tight reach.

GOOSEWINGING

A radical move that sometimes works (although I've never tried it), is to 'goosewing' the gennaker on the opposite side to the boom and run dead downwind. A friend of mine who races J/80 keelboats says that sometimes you can gain a tactical advantage heading for a leeward mark, and gain the inside overlap on another boat that puts into two gybes. It's an interesting manoeuvre to experiment with, although I've never seen it attempted in a planing skiff. If you're sailing in displacement mode, particularly in a heavy keelboat, then the shorter distance of sailing dead downwind might just pay off. And as my mate points out, it could earn you inside overlap at a leeward mark. Let me know how you get on!

Great Boathandling Makes for Great Tactics

Stevie Morrison and Ben Rhodes won the 49er Worlds in Cascais 2007. One race in particular was really whacky, with wildly shifting and gusting breeze, but somehow Stevie and Ben got their heads around it. Great boathandling enabled them to make some great tactical calls. Stevie looks back on a crazy race that went almost perfectly.

'The race course was right under the shore at Cascais so very shifty, gusting between 6 and 20 knots. I remember it being a moment on the first beat where the wind had shifted left, then really hard right, and I just said to Ben: "Look, we're just going to point at the mark and see which way the wind takes us for a moment." We were pretty much aimed straight at the windward mark with sails in the middle of the boat and lying in about 10th place and like "Oh blimey, this is going to be quite a race."

'A couple of good little shifts later, and we were 3rd or 4th at the windward mark. I always remember down the first run we found a gust there when we needed it,

Stevie Morrison and Ben Rhodes on their way to winning the 49er Worlds in Cascais

and obviously there's an element of luck to that. Ben and I managed to just hit that gust and did about seven or eight gybes down the first run. We went straight down the middle of the run, kind of bouncing off the other boats that were ahead of us, and by the leeward mark we were probably a good 200 metres ahead of the second place boat, which was obviously pretty nice.

'It was a three-lap race and we just seemed to hit pretty much every shift. What I remember most fondly about the whole thing – and this will probably come back to bite me in the bum one day – but was as we were going down the third run, we took a little gust and we went past Nathan Outteridge [multiple World Champion from Australia]. We lapped Nathan as he was coming down to the finish, I think he still finished 10th or 11th in the race and still ended up with a bronze medal at that Worlds. So certainly I wouldn't look down on him too much, but for a guy that's as talented as him, to have lapped him was a pretty fond memory that I can assure you doesn't get left in the closet. He is reminded of that on a regular basis!

'Looking back on it, I think our philosophy of tacking when the jib flapped worked well for us. And downwind in a 49er you can get a gust and if you use it right you can stay with it for pretty much the whole leg. I think where we did a good job in that race – and what's pretty key in a fast asymmetric boat – is having that ability to make sure you don't sail yourself off a gust and into a lull.

'Having the boathandling skills to put in six or seven gybes in a two or three minute run, that's the main lesson. It's really important to have the boathandling to keep clinging on to that gust. So as soon as we even had a hint of the wind going at all light, we were gybing straight back across the gust. You've got to have the boathandling skills to be able to throw in as many gybes as you need if it's appropriate.'

CHAPTER 4

SURVIVAL SAILING

Once you've got the basic manoeuvres squared away in light-to-medium winds, you can then start looking at wrestling the boat around the race course in strong winds. Sailing high-performance boats in big wind and waves is not for the faint-hearted, but then you're not one of the faint-hearted, are you! Let's kick off with one of the biggest manoeuvres of all, bearing away in a big breeze. . .

Extreme Bear-Away

Bearing away from a beat onto a downwind course can be very challenging in high-speed skiffs and multihulls. We've already mentioned the danger of the 'death zone' in the previous chapter. Well, this manoeuvre takes you right through that zone, so the key is to minimise the time you spend there. In a 49er – one of the most difficult skiffs to bear away in a breeze – the key is to go from upwind to downwind in the shortest possible time.

The nose buries as Chris Draper and Simon Hiscocks turn their 49er downwind

As you approach the windward mark, release the vang to its downwind position, get the jib out of the cleat ready to ease. Just before the crucial moment, get to the back of the boat, with the windward wing down flat to the water, one foot in the footloop for the helm, ease the jib and pull her away. But don't even think about bearing away unless the boat is flat or slightly heeled to windward. If it's not, bail out, get yourself ready again, and start from the beginning. Even if you're sailing well above the windward mark by this stage, it's better to go the extra distance rather than lose patience and fall in.

As for who takes the mainsheet at this stage, it's whatever you feel more comfortable with. As the helm I like to take the mainsheet for the manoeuvre, but it's personal preference.

One universal rule: be committed to it. It's about clear communication, and you might even count down into the bear-away. Waves are an issue, so better to sail on a reach to sail clear of other boats, before you do the manoeuvre. The bear-away and the kite hoist are totally separate manoeuvres, so treat them as such. Wait for your moment before you hoist the kite.

Commit to the bear-away, and tell the boat who's boss

Extreme Conditions

Straight line survival with the gennaker

Getting downwind in big breeze with the gennaker can be scary if you let the boat run away with itself. In most boats, you're trying to drive them as hard as possible all the time, but if you do that in high performance skiffs or multihulls there's a danger of nosediving and pitchpoling, sending you flying over the front of the boat – or worse, into the rig.

If you're sailing significantly faster than the waves, then you're at risk of nosediving. At this point you should treat the gennaker sheet as the throttle on the engine. The closer you set the gennaker to optimum trim, the faster you will go and the more risk you are taking. So you have two options: oversheet the kite or flap it.

If you are consistently too fast, then oversheet the kite as much as you need to feel comfortable. The more you oversheet, the slower the boat will go.

If you're worried about nosediving, curl the gennaker or oversheet it

If you can cope with max speed most of the time, and it's just the occasional wave where you think you could come to grief, then flap the gennaker until you've overtaken the wave and the moment of danger has passed. Then oversheet the kite and get going again.

Keep the mainsheet on fairly tight. With a masthead rigged asymmetric, the mainsail leech will help support the mast and work as a form of backstay. But even if you're sailing a boat that doesn't have a full-hoist gennaker, keeping the mainsail sheeted in will stop the top of the leech leaning over the front of the boat. This will help reduce the tendency of the rig to drive the bow down, and the boat will feel safer and easier to steer.

Expert Advice

Darren Bundock, high-performance multihulls

Downwind in extreme conditions, I feel safer flying the kite because it actually lifts the nose a little bit. The main priority is always to keep the crew out on trapeze and right out the back of the boat. Don't back off too much, keep driving the boat. I find that it's when I try to take it easy and the crew sits in – that's when you generally get into trouble because the boat wants to nosedive a lot more than if the crew's at the back

Ragging the kite on a Tornado

and you are still pushing the boat moderately hard. It's easier to get downwind in the modern Tornado with a gennaker than it was in the old days when it was just a main and jib boat.

Sometimes ragging the gennaker helps, especially if you think you're going to plough into the back of the next wave. I think the helm can do a lot here. If you're going down the back of a wave and you think you're going to plough into the next one, just doing a short little luff-up can lift the nose up and around, over the top of the next wave. It's a hard technique to come to terms with because, as you round up, the boat actually powers up. It takes some balls to get into that technique because everything's telling you to bear away, but bearing away will actually make it worse.

Rick Perkins, Musto Skiff

In the Musto Skiff, and in other asymmetrics, there are some key things to do to ensure you don't go over the handle bars. Firstly it's just looking ahead. Obviously you've got to look at the kite, trim it, but after a while you kind of get a good feel for that. So when you're travelling flat out, it's about looking ahead at the waves ahead of you and picking the route through which you're going to sail. If you see a particularly nasty wave-set, slowing the boat down is going to help you negotiate it.

(Continued)

In some classes there is a preference for flogging the kite rather than overtrimming it. That's fine in a doublehanded asymmetric where the crew can use both hands to get the kite back on after it's had a flap. In a Musto Skiff, obviously, you're steering with one hand so moving large amounts of kite sheet with your front hand isn't very easy. It's much better to actually oversheet so that the process of getting going again doesn't require pulling in 3 or 4 metres of sheet – which is very difficult to do one-handed.

Think about how you've got your mainsail trimmed. If the mainsail's not trimmed in enough, if it's out by the shroud, the top of the mainsail is very square to the centreline and it's pushing the bow down. That's going to make you more prone to pitchpoling.

Keep the boat flat. If it's heeled it's more likely to trip over or for a wing to catch a wave, so keep the boat flat, mainsail trimmed on, look at where you're going through the waves and don't be afraid to slow yourself down. It's much better to slow down and perhaps lose a bit of speed every now and then, than to capsize with the kite up.

Survival Sailing *without* the Gennaker

In a lot of asymmetrics it's easier getting downwind in survival conditions with the kite hoisted. The sail provides extra lift to the bow, and if you do nosedive, the water has a much clearer run through the boat and the empty chute. With the kite in the chute, any water rushing over the

Getting downwind without the kite can be even more challenging. . .

bow has a much harder time moving through the cockpit, the resistance builds up and . . . over you go.

That said, in extreme conditions, getting the kite up in the first place is easier said than done. And, in any case, you need to know how to get downwind without the kite for getting position for the pre-start and other situations outside of racing. You need to know how to get safely downwind without the gennaker.

Oversheet the mainsail

As we mentioned in the previous section, the problems arise when the boat is travelling faster than the waves, setting up a perfect scenario for a nosedive. So the answer is to try to match wave speed. How to achieve this? By oversheeting the mainsail. If you are running downwind and you have the boom out to the shroud, you are presenting maximum sail area to the wind. By pulling

The mainsail is well sheeted in, but with the crew dropping the kite, the mainsail will load up quickly. This team is just about getting away with it

in the mainsail, then, you are effectively reducing sail area. In other words, oversheeting is a very crude form of reefing. Crude, but effective.

Steer across the waves

The other thing you can do is to always steer across the waves, never directly into the back of them. Mimic a Laser, which alternates between broad reaching across the wave, and then bearing away until it's running by the lee. This will mean the wind is blowing from leech to luff of the mainsail, and you are not far from a gybe. So this method is not without its risks, but it might be preferable to constantly spearing into the back of the next wave and pitchpoling.

Survival Gybe

In survival conditions, where just getting around the racecourse is a victory in itself, then it's worth knowing a gybing technique which certainly has served me well in 49ers and International 14s and probably applies to most high-performance asymmetrics.

In really strong winds, any gybe where you stay upright is a good gybe!

The modification from a standard gybe is very simple. The entry is exactly the same – it's all about keeping maximum speed on as long as possible into the manoeuvre. Remember, the faster you are, the safer you'll be.

For the crew, everything else is the same as a standard gybe except that as you go into the gybe and the crew runs through the boat, you just keep on hauling on the old kite sheet and keep it pinned in.

When you come out of the gybe onto the new side, you're now looking at the strange sight of a tightly strapped gennaker with the wind blowing across it from back to front, i.e. from leech to luff. It might look weird, but you'll find you can actually steer out of the gybe onto your new heading in a very controlled manner.

The nice thing about it is that while the boat went through the gybe quickly (which is the safest way), it's now travelling quite slowly, which means the boat isn't leaping from wave top to wave top as quickly as it might be if the gennaker was set for maximum speed. This gives you ample opportunity to get hooked up onto the trapeze and into your footstraps.

Once you've settled and you're ready to hit hyperspace, the crew releases the old kite sheet, the gennaker blows past the forestay, and you can set the kite again for maximum speed. Or at least as much speed the conditions will allow.

The RS200 has a big mainsail and small gennaker, so get the kite filling and powered up as fast as possible out of the gybe

Warning to hiking sailors

I asked Geoff Carveth and Dave Hivey how they thought this technique would apply to slower asymmetrics like RS200s and RS400s, and they didn't reckon it would work. First, you don't have the same righting moment available, as there are no trapezes; and second, the kite is relatively small compared with the mainsail. Both experts reckon you want to get the kite gybed and set as soon as possible out of the manoeuvre, to get the boat up to speed and get the pressure off the mainsail. They thought that trying this 'safety gybe' could result in a broach. But for trapeze skiffs with masthead gennakers, I can't recommend the technique highly enough.

Expert Advice

Safety gybing with Trevor Baylis

Gybing technique is one of the toughest and most critical elements of skiff sailing, but Trevor Baylis (world champion in 14s, 18s and 505) has some ideas that will help make heavy-air gybing a whole lot safer. . .

In high winds, move through the boat as fast as possible, and worry about setting the kite afterwards

Verbal guarantee

'One thing I will say to my helmsman in fresh conditions is: "I will be out on the wire on the other side. Don't stop the turn." A lot of helms S-turn out of the exit, but this is where you can start to get in trouble. It's much more comforting for the helm to know he can keep on steering high out of the gybe, knowing that you're going to be on the wire for him. Even if you can't guarantee that you'll have the kite set, at least you'll be in the wire.

'There have been some occasions where it's been so windy that I've not even bothered picking up the new kite sheet. At the International 14 World Championships in Bermuda, we had the sea wall at the leeward mark and waves coming back at you, and we knew that if we capsized there would be a high chance of breaking the mast. So we just had to be really conservative. We just crossed the boat, we'd both come out with the kite flogging, and get our feet in the foot loops. The boat wouldn't be going that fast, but we'd be pretty safe. Zach would get settled, and then I'd reach forward and pick up the sheet, set the kite and get going again. If you haven't tried it, you'll be amazed just how stable the boat is even with the kite flogging like that.'

Tacking

Part of what makes lightweight skiffs so attractive – their light weight, that is – is also what makes them a real beast when trying to tack them in strong winds. With a lack of hull weight, the boat stops easily, particularly with all the wind resistance and drag of a big, fully-battened rig as it starts to flog. The boat slows down easily and, if you hang around too long during the tack, it can stop altogether or start going backwards. I've even seen a B14 capsizing backwards, bow over stern!

Half way through a windy tack, the boat is at risk of becoming very unstable and unpredictable. Just as a fast gybe is a safe gybe, the same is true of tacking a high-performance skiff. Coming into a tack, aim to sail the boat totally flat, steering slowly into it. The more controlled your entry, the better your exit. If you go through too heeled, it swings through too quickly on the new tack, or refuses to tack at all. Getting blown into leeward on the new tack is the most common problem, so you might have to watch the crew and see how quickly they react. Be ready to let the jib go if they are slow getting on to the new side. The helm's priority is steering and, as long as he holds it head to wind long enough to give the crew time to move to the new side, you should be fine.

Get the skiff through the eye of the wind before it loses too much speed and stalls

If you have a self-tacking jib, ease the sheet six inches before the tack, this will give the helm a wider steering groove out of the tack. Oversteering out of the tack with a tightly pinned jib is sure to capsize you.

In a singlehanded skiff like the Musto Skiff, you have no jib to help pull the bow away from the breeze. The important thing here is to maintain enough speed to drive the boat all the way through the turn and out on to a close reach. Don't even think about pointing up on the new heading until you've got the boat moving on a close reach. As always, the key to getting through the tack is a flat and fast boat, and when you don't have a jib this becomes even more important.

In waves, look for a flat spot in which to complete your tack. Be clear with your commands, and when you go for it you've got to be committed to it.

CHAPTER 5

AVOIDING DISASTER

All sailboat racing is about minimising your mistakes. The sailor that makes the least mistakes is the winner. It might seem a negative way of looking at things, but it's still quite a useful one. And it's particularly relevant to high performance boats that are difficult to sail. In strong winds, if you can avoid all the big mistakes – e.g. capsizing, collisions, pitchpoles and so on – then you'll probably do very well.

In this chapter we look at some of the biggest mistakes, and how to avoid them.

Make a Plan

First, let's talk about a general philosophy; about knowing what you're about, and what your aims are. In team boats, this is particularly important. Everyone on board needs to know what the game plan is before you start, in fact before you even go afloat. As former 49er World medallist, 505 World Champion and America's Cup veteran Morgan Larson puts it: 'Even a bad plan is better than no plan. Of course if I get a bad start – which I often do – then you need a Plan B, of course!' Not that Morgan does get many bad starts, but I hope you understand the point. A boat, and a team, that knows where it's going, is much more likely to get there!

Discuss your plan before the race: Olympic 49er Champions Iker Martinez and Xabi Fernandez, deep in thought

Prepare for the Unexpected

This follows on from the previous point, and is one of the most overlooked aspects of sailing.

When you go out and practise, it's too easy just to go through the standard manoeuvres such as tacking and gybing, and maybe some mark roundings. But what about practising for when things go wrong, such as 720 penalty turns and capsizes? The best way to practise is to put yourself in these pressure situations, and see how you respond.

The other classic thing in many asymmetric and one-design classes, which do nearly all their racing on windward/leeward courses, is not to bother how to two-sail reach because you never have to do it. Then, one day, when the wind shifts and the course gets all skewed, suddenly you have to start two-sail reaching, which is the toughest point of sailing in a boat like the 49er. Times like these really reveal which teams have been putting in the practice for those rare eventualities – and which ones haven't.

The other common mistake is only to practise bear-aways on starboard tack, because that is what you normally do on a port-rounding course. Bearing away in a 49er is a pretty tough

Roger Gilbert & Ben McGrane on an 'untypical' port bear-away in the International 14

exercise in strong winds. It's easy to pitchpole or capsize if you get your timing wrong, so teams practise their bearing-away until it works like clockwork. However, try bearing away on the other gybe – and it feels totally alien. This is what Chris Draper and Simon Hiscocks discovered in the build-up to the Athens Olympics, when they struggled to bear the boat away on port during an important race in big winds.

So, after getting home from the regatta, Chris and Simon went out into Weymouth Bay and put a hard training session in, purely to conquer this one manoeuvre. It didn't take them long before the port bear-away felt like second nature, and it was another weapon in their armoury. Whether they've had to use it in anger since then, I don't know. Probably not very often, if at all, but the strangest things often happen at the most crucial of moments.

And I do remember seeing one race at Athens where the wind shifted massively, putting all the 49ers on to a very tight gennaker reach. Unfamiliar territory for all but the most prepared of teams, who made hay while others made a hash of getting through the leeward gate in good shape.

Trawling the Kite

Trawling the kite is a horrible feeling. It can happen when you're hoisting the gennaker but then part of the sail flops into the water and then the next moment the whole thing is in the sea, trawling like a fisherman's net.

At this point of the hoist, the crew must pull like mad to avoid the dreaded 'trawl'

The boat slows to a near standstill, and puts massive strain on the sail, and the mast. If the sail has completely fallen in the water, you will need to turn up into the wind and stop the boat completely. Then the crew will need to reach over the side and manhandle the soggy sail back on to the deck, and ideally stow it in the bag or chute before you get going again.

Sometimes, if just one corner of the sail falls into the water, there's a chance of saving yourself from trawling humiliation by powering through the rest of the hoist as quickly as possible.

Expert Advice

Steve Irish: Avoiding the trawl

For another perspective, we asked former RS800 champion Steve Irish about the dreaded trawl, and how to avoid it.

Leeward heel is the main reason why the trawl happens. So, from a helming point of view, you've got to make sure you do bear away far enough that you've got the boat slightly over on top – and that just gives the kite that little bit of air before it has a chance to hit the water. Make sure that the crew doesn't rush into the hoist too much. They've got to be ready. At the start of the hoist they've got to be fully solid in the bottom of the boat and once they start the hoist that it's one continuous movement and doesn't get stopped at any point. A lot of trawls tend to happen when the crew started the hoist because they're desperate to get it going – and then find they have to reposition or stop. Then the kite just droops slightly, catches the water and suddenly the job becomes twice as hard.

On the sea, the helm should be looking for the right wave so, when you call the hoist, you should be happy that you can sit on the face of one wave for the whole of the hoist. You're also looking then just to keep a real constant heel angle, so the crew's balance isn't being knocked at all. If you can do that, then you should be perfectly alright. If we did start to get a trawl in the RS800, I'd shout at my crew to 'pull it hard,' and he was usually big enough that he could normally rip it back out of the water without it developing into a full-on trawl.

Twist in the Kite

If the gennaker goes up with an 'hourglass' twist, then you need to pay attention to how the kite is stowed during the drops. Keeping some tension in the gennaker sheet will make it much harder for the kite to twist on the way into the bag or chute. It's when you let the kite flog before you drop it that the problems occur. So keeping sheet tension on as late as possible is the key to twist prevention.

But what if the kite has twisted? Try the following remedies, in this order:

- Oversheet the gennaker, pulling it all the way in, then releasing, and pulling all the way in again. Sometimes the kite can untwist itself just by doing this, but if the kite is still twisted . . .
- Ease the halyard half a metre on a dinghy, by a metre or more on a sportsboat, then try over-sheeting again. As soon as the kite untwists, rehoist the halyard. However, if the kite is still twisted . . .
- Gybe, keeping as much tension on the old sheet as possible. The act of gybing will shake out all but the very worst of twists.

Trying to untwist the kite on a Rebel Skiff

If none of these remedies works, then this really is a major twist, and you may well need to drop the gennaker to the deck and manually untwist the sail. But this doesn't happen very often.

Expert Tip

Geoff Carveth: Getting a twist out of an SB20 kite

The bowman runs to leeward, grabs the clew of the gennaker and pulls hard down the leech. The helmsman steers slightly hotter to put more pressure in the kite. If this doesn't work, then ease the halyard a few feet and then try doing the first two things again. As soon as the kite untwists, rehoist the sail and sheet on. But if none of this works, then you'll need to gybe.

Twisted SB20 gennaker: this might require easing the halyard a few feet, or even a gybe

Keep a Lookout Downwind

With most modern gennakers setting quite close to the water, this can create a large blind spot to leeward when you're travelling downwind. Some classes like the Melges 24 permit windows in the gennaker, but on many classes you have to find other ways of keeping an eye out downwind.

When both of you are on a trapeze in an International 14 or a 49er for example, it's very difficult to know what's going on ahead and to leeward of you. One thing you can do is to sail the boat very flat, or almost heel to windward, provided that you're very low on the trapeze. But, in light-to-medium conditions, this isn't always practical. So it could be that either the helm or the crew needs to move to leeward occasionally, just to get a sense of where the boats are on the upwind leg, so that you know if there's a possibility that you might be on a collision course and you can do something about it.

You might also hope that the boat coming upwind will give adequate notice by hailing to you and making you aware of the fact that they are there. Self preservation might suggest that that would be the sensible thing to do but, in my experience, this does not always happen, whether

A very useful window in a Melges 24 gennaker, but most asymmetrics don't have this luxury

COLLISION COURSE? OVERSHEET THE KITE

If you're sailing downwind on port gybe in a good puff, and you find yourself on a collision course with a boat on starboard, what do you do? Most people gybe, which is fine if that's what you want to do anyway. But what if you're already on the favoured gybe and want to continue on port?

Sheet in the gennaker as hard as possible and the boat will slow down significantly. Let the starboard boat pass safely in front, then release the sheet until the gennaker is setting nicely again. Yes, you've given away ground, but you've maintained control over your tactics rather than being dictated to by the other boat.

Helmsman has stepped in and oversheeted the kite to slow the boat down rather than gybe

it's because the other sailors feel intimidated by the sight of a fast asymmetric coming towards them, or they don't feel the need to tell you. There's certainly no onus under the racing rules for them to tell you, so get in the habit of looking to leeward every minute or so.

Taking Penalties

RS200 champion Dave Hivey practises his penalties. Most good sailors do:

'It's a good boathandling exercise anyway. The general rule is tack first when you're sailing upwind and gybe first when you're heading downwind. When you're doing the turn – whether it's a 360 or 720 turn – make sure that you keep the mainsheet playing the whole way through the gybe. You've got to sheet really hard, really fast on the mainsheet as you're spinning the boat into the wind to get that drive from the leech of the mainsail. That will get you safely through the tack, at which point you ease the jib and mainsail as you bear away straight into a gybe.

'Equally important is paying attention to the heel of the boat. Whenever you're turning into the wind, the boat should be heeled away from you, and whenever you're turning away from the wind, the boat's got to be heeled over on top of you.

Dave Hivey practises 360 turns in case he gets a penalty during racing

You've got to make sure that you keep to that rule all the way through and then the boat will keep spinning through the turn. If you ever let the heel go the wrong way at any point, the boat is in danger of stalling.'

As Dave says, focusing on accurate sheeting and heel angle are the keys to successful penalty turns, and they're well worth practising.

Capsizing

The next chapter is about one of the most common mistakes – capsizing. It's a big subject all by itself, which is why we've separated it into its own chapter.

CHAPTER 6

BROACHING & CAPSIZING

All sailing boats broach. Fortunately, with keelboats, it stops there. With dinghies and multihulls, however, the broach is merely the aperitif before the main course: the capsize.

Capsizing

Just like any dinghy, an asymmetric modern dinghy is quite capable of capsizing, and some of the high performance ones are more prone to capsizing than most.

You can see this when you launch a boat like a 49er or a Musto Skiff or an International 14. You can't just hold onto it at the bow by the forestay and expect the boat to stay upright by itself like you'd expect a Fireball or a Laser to stay upright, for example. High performance skiffs naturally want to fall over because they're narrow on the waterline and they have tall rigs.

So you're dealing with something that's inherently unstable, although it's a little bit like a bicycle. The more speed you have going forwards, the more stable the boat tends to become.

Keelboats may broach, but at least they don't fully capsize (not very often, anyway!)

That's the thing to bear in mind whenever you're sailing the boat – if you can keep the speed on through a manoeuvre, you have a much better chance of staying upright.

Why Capsizes Happen

Gybing

One of the most common places for a capsize, like any other dinghy, is in a gybe, particularly when it's windy. We've already said that it's very important to keep an asymmetric dinghy upright at all times. Rolling the boat to windward in a gybe is not a good thing, unless the wind is really light and you're looking for some roll to help flick the battens through the gybe.

If you do capsize, it could be for a number of reasons. Beginners tend to apply too much rudder to the turn, turning far too quickly, in too tight an arc. This creates a momentum in the top of the rig which is hard to fight. After you've capsized a few times doing this, you'll soon

Crossing the boat too late is a common cause of capsizing

Broaching after a gybe in the SB20

understand what I mean and you'll start using the rudder much less than perhaps you did initially. If you do capsize to windward after a gybe, the chances are that you'll end up in the water next to the boom.

Another danger spot on the race course is at the leeward mark. If you round up quickly and with the boat slightly heeled to leeward, it can be very difficult coping with the sudden increase in power. Getting thrown in to leeward is the risk here.

Dealing with sudden gusts and lulls, or big wind shifts, is a challenge. If you sail into a lull or a header, the boat can come on top of you and capsize to windward. Unhooking from the trapeze can unweight the boat and if you're lucky the wind will blow the boat upright again. Of course you've now got to haul yourself back into the boat, but this is preferable to a total capsize.

In strong winds there's the risk of the pitchpole, capsizing over the bow. We've already looked at that, flapping the kite and other slowing down techniques. But every so often you'll get it wrong, and the capsize will be inevitable.

Nosediving

Almost any boat is capable of capsizing sideways. High performance skiffs and multihulls offer the additional fun of capsizing forwards, a.k.a. the nosedive! Sometimes you can survive it, after

you've witnessed 'green water' washing over the bow and through the cockpit. But sometimes you have to accept that the nosedive is just one of those things that comes as part and parcel of high performance sailing.

OK, So You've Capsized. What Now?

Safety first

Much of what you do next depends on the particular characteristics of your boat. First thing to do is to make sure that you and your crew are clear of any ropes and, particularly, that your trapeze hooks are not tangled up with anything. If they are, then getting untangled is the top priority. If swimming clear isn't possible, then be ready to cut the tangled line or the trapeze harness if necessary. For this reason I strongly advise you to keep a knife on board. On the 18ft skiff class, having a knife attached to the aft port trapeze rack is a class rule, so that in the event of a capsize and one of the crew being caught in the water, anyone will know where to find a knife, even one of the rescue boats. This is a great example to follow and all high performance sailors should do it.

First check everyone's OK

Avoid the 'turtle'

When you're sure that everyone is clear of the rigging and people are free to move in the water, your next priority should be to prevent the boat from going turtle, i.e. from turning upside down. This might involve one or both of you going straight round to the daggerboard and catching the boat before it inverts completely.

Bag the kite

If you're confident that your kind of boat is not so prone to inverting and you think you've got time to get the gennaker back into its chute while the boat is still on its side, then this is the next priority. So, when you stabilise the boat and you're sure that it's going to stay on its side, get the kite back into the chute. If you find that you're struggling to get it back in, firstly check that the halyard is uncleated. If you have a jib, pull the jib in quite hard, so that there's a hard

Close to turning turtle - ie upside down - which will make getting the boat upright even longer and more arduous

surface for the kite to bear against and this will minimise the danger of the kite wrapping itself around the forestay.

In singlehanded boats such as Musto Skiffs, the lack of a jib can be a problem, making it more likely for the kite to twist around the forestay. Having a newer kite with stiffer cloth tends to be less prone to wrapping itself around the wire. So, alongside the benefits of a newer sail being slightly faster and easier to get in and out of the chute and through racing manoeuvres, another good reason is your ability to retrieve the kite safely.

Getting upright

When you've got the chute back in, now you can start thinking about bringing the boat upright. Some boats respond well to having lots of vang and cunningham pulled on to the mainsail,

The boat comes upright, but that doesn't always mean you're home and dry . . .

because this flattens it off and makes it more easy for the water to flow off the sail, making it much easier to pull the boat upright. Experiment with different tensions in these controls until you find what works best for your type of boat. You'll be surprised how much difference these sail controls can make.

When you're ready to pull the boat upright, make sure that the mainsheet is uncleated and (once the kite is stowed in the chute) that the jib is also uncleated. It can pay to keep the jib loosely sheeted and then release the cleat at the last moment when you believe that the boat is actually coming upright, because a loose jib lying around in the water can wrap itself around the forestay. In the case of a fully battened jib, you can end up with broken battens, so keeping the jib tensioned for as long as possible will help minimise sail damage.

The next thing to decide is which way up the boat is going to come in relation to the wind. A lot of boats when they're in the water tend to rotate around until the mast is facing upwind. A 49er is one such boat, and this means that as you manage to pull the mast tip out of the water, the wind will gradually catch underneath the underside of the sail until the wind lifts the sail up and flips it upright with some force. The most likely outcome is that the wind will flip it all the way over, and capsize the boat to leeward. This gives you another capsize to recover from, so here's the technique for preventing the 'double capsize'.

Preventing the boat from flipping

First you need to have helm and crew standing on the board. As the boat comes upright and as the mast tip shows signs of wanting to lift from the water, the lighter of the two of you should jump down into the water between the gap between the deck and the boom. The helmsman or whoever has gone into the water, clips onto the helm's trapeze ring which is

Maximum effort now could save you having to endure a secondary capsize

lying in the water, grabs hold of the mainsheet without tensioning it, grabs hold of the tiller and waits for the crew to pull the mast out of the water. As the mast blows upright, the sailor attached to the trapeze wire needs to stay put, keeping your bottom sitting on what will now be the new windward rack. With the speed that the boat comes upright, it can be unnerving going through this process, but you'll find that the end result is surprisingly calm with the boat settling back in upright mode. Most of the time you will avoid the follow-on capsize to leeward because your weight has counteracted the force of the boat being blown over to leeward.

If, however, it's really windy and you do feel the boat going the other way, if you're quick enough, you can jump onto the trapeze and apply more righting moment to stop this happening. If the boat continues to capsize, then be ready to jump out the back of the boat beyond the mainsail. Fall from that height into the mainsail, and you may will put a sailor-shaped hole in it! So make sure you leap before you fall.

Hey, if you're going to capsize, you might as well look like you meant it! *(Continued)*

Helm and crew work together on the daggerboard until the mast and sails are lying flat on the water. Then the crew (being the heavier) stays on the board while the helm swims round to the cockpit... *(Continued)*

With the mast pointing towards the wind, once the wind gets under the sails the boat comes upright very quickly, so the crew moves fast to get on board while he can. . .
(Continued)

Nicely done! The helm stabilised the boat sufficiently for the nimble crew to get on board, avoiding a follow-on capsize, which would have been the result if they hadn't been so fast to act, although. . . *(Continued)*

Not home and dry quite yet! The crew is still in front of the mast and needs to get aft at the first opportunity. From there he can join his helm on the wing and help get the boat moving again.

The Eskimo roll

If it's really windy or the technique above doesn't work, then one of you needs to commit to the cause a little more. Whoever has been standing on the board to get the mast out of the water now needs to commit to the 'Eskimo roll'. As the boat comes upright, grab on to the board and stay with it. This means you're going underwater, but most likely not for long.

The Eskimo roll may sound unpleasant, but it's really not that bad. Your body resistance and your body weight helps slow down the rate of turn and reduces the likelihood of the boat doing a further capsize, so if the crew holds onto the centreboard until such time as the boat settles down in an upright position, you can push yourself out from underneath the boat and come up to one or other of the gunnels and work out which side of the boat you should get back into.

If it's windy, or you don't manage to control the rate of turn and the boat does capsize, at least you're right there next to the daggerboard clinging on to it. If you've been really smart you might have rotated yourself up onto the new topside of the daggerboard, already applying your weight to the board and ready to pull the boat up before the mast tip dips in the water again.

If this second capsize does occur, you should be able to recover from it because the mast won't have had time to fill up with water and the sails won't have had time to get waterlogged, So, if you're quick, you can still pull the boat upright from this second capsize quite quickly and effectively. Now with the wind on your back as you're standing on the daggerboard, it may help to release the vang and take some of the tension out of the mainsail leech.

Another tip: if you're lacking righting moment and you're standing on the daggerboard trying to get the mast out of the water, use the control line tails or spinnaker sheets to step towards the end of the board. Remember also that this extra leverage also puts additional strain on the board, so be careful if you're racing with a lightly built foil. A broken board will make it much harder to get the boat upright, let alone what it will be like to sail with.

The other thing to remember when you're bringing your boat upright, is to try to keep your trapeze hook away from the hull and away from the daggerboard, because it's easy to put dents in the hull and even easier to take chunks out of the fine trailing edge of the daggerboard. For this reason, it's wise to pull yourself up over the front edge of the board, so that if your hook does come into contact with the leading edge, it's unlikely to do as much damage on that side of the board.

Righting from inversion

If the boat does invert, then there's a further stage that you need to get to before you go through all the steps described in the previous section.

When the boat is upside down, the hull is going to come up most easily onto its side by standing on the downwind gunnel or rack. Grasp the top of the daggerboard and try leaning back away from the daggerboard to leeward. As the boat starts coming upright the wind should catch the underside of the hull and, if you've got solid or netted wings like a 49er or B14, the wind will catch the underside of the wings which act as a sail to start helping the boat come upright.

If the boat turns turtle, then the work load increases

What if the mast is touching the bottom?

If, however, you've capsized in shallow water and you can feel or hear the mast grating on the ground, don't get on the boat, because that would just put more load on the mast. At this point the mast is very fragile and any further pressure on the mast could result in it breaking. The best thing that you can do at this stage is to help speed up the rotation of the hull around the mast until the hull is downwind and, if there's current, down tide of current. This will mean that any current and/or wind is helping push the boat downwind and helping lift the mast away from the sea bed. As soon as the boat has rotated to leeward of the mast, gently put some weight on the daggerboard and see if the boat wants to come upright.

If you can sense that it's still not wanting to come upright, then wait a little bit longer and if you think it's not going to come upright, you might want to wait for help from a rescue boat to help tow the mast tip out of the mud, or whatever it is that the mast is stuck in. Once the mast has come clear of the mud, then you can proceed to righting the boat in the usual way.

DON'T FALL INTO THE MAINSAIL!

The first time I capsized a 49er, I jumped into the mainsail, and a split-second later, I'd jumped through it! Very embarrassing, and rather expensive. If you've reached the point of no-return, accept the fact and plan your exit and jump – not into the mast, not into the mainsail, but straight into the water!

Expert Advice

Rick Perkins, skiff sailing

Right the boat with the kite up?

If you capsize in light-to-medium airs, you might be able to get the boat upright with the gennaker still hoisted. If you can get away with it, you'll be up and running much quicker than if you spend time with the boat on its side while you get the kite back into the chute. In stronger winds there are no short cuts, but it's worth experimenting with what you can get away with in light winds.

(Continued)

Geoff Carveth, sportsboat sailing

How do I get out of a broach?

1. Ease a metre or more of kite sheet
2. Ease the vang
3. Drop the kite halyard by 2 metres.

Generally these three things will get you upright. Once the boat comes up, hoist the kite back up to the top, get settled on a downwind course, sheet on and go. Don't do it again!

Glenn Ashby, high performance catamaran

Getting a cat up the right way

Glenn Ashby admits to having capsized a few catamarans in his time, although not when he's won one of his many world titles in boats like the A-Class, the Formula 18 and the Tornado, of course . . .

> If you can keep the boat on its side with the rig pointing towards the wind, it's a pretty good start. But if the boat does go turtle and you are completely upside down, getting to the back leeward corner of the boat is quite a good one. What that actually does is pick up the bow of the boat and get a bit of air under the trampoline of the boat. So you pretty much lean back in the leeward rudder.

Getting the bows facing towards the wind will make it much easier to right the boat

Once the boat starts to come up at a bit of an angle, hold on to the righting line and start working your way forward, while the rig starts to come up to horizontal. Move your body weight forward, almost up near the bow.

The trampoline will act like a sail and pivot the boat around, so the bow will stay upwind. The back of the boat will start swinging downwind and the leading edge of the mast will be almost 90 degrees to the wind. So when you flick the boat upright again it's almost like doing a water start on a sailboard. When the wind catches the rig, it will force the mast out of the water. This means you're just using your bodyweight to flick the boat back upright, and the rig is working for you. Having the bow slightly forward into the breeze

The trampoline acts like a sail and pivots the boat around.

(Continued)

and the mast slightly aft of 90 degrees makes it really easy to flick the boat up again.

"If you had the kite up when you capsized, get it in the bag or chute before you attempt to right the boat, unless it's really light airs when you might get away with it staying hoisted."

CHAPTER 7

BOAT SPEED

Because asymmetric boats are so dynamic and responsive, they are quite good at telling you when they feel right.

Use the Force (in the rudder)

One of the best indicators in any boat is what you feel through the rudder. It should feel balanced. When the kite is oversheeted, you can feel the lee helm in the rudder. Ease the sheet to the point of the gennaker luff curling, and you'll feel the rudder becoming more balanced.

Experiment with different mainsail trim, and see what effect it has on the rudder. Ease the main and you should feel the lee helm increase. Tighten the main and you'll feel the lee helm

The helmsman can feel how the boat is going through the feedback from the tiller

disappear again. This is why you see asymmetrics sailing around with the mainsail on or near the centreline downwind, because it's helping bring the rudder into balance.

The rudder is your best feedback tool on the boat.

Which Mode Should I Be In?

We've mentioned the difference between 'soaking' and 'planing' a few times. It's hard to set some general rules for every kind of asymmetric boat, but let's look again at the basic principles. Top 49er sailor and Olympic coach, Paul Brotherton, has an interesting way of determining which mode you should be in.

Determine your mode by whether you being driven mainly by true wind or apparent wind

'The important thing to understand with asymmetric rigs is when you are being blown along by the wind and when you are sailing under apparent wind. The crossover is quite stark, and calls for different techniques. One of the best ways to tell whether you are apparent wind sailing or being blown by the real wind is to pull the mainsail in. If there is an immediate and large effect, then you are apparent wind sailing. If not, then you are being blown by the breeze.'

In something like an RS400 you are being blown along by the breeze up to about 10 or 12 knots of true wind. This means that if you are on a run, you want to aim deep downwind with the bowsprit well pulled back [the RS400 has a swinging bowsprit], as heading up will not give you enough extra speed to justify the extra distance you will sail.

This situation changes dramatically at 10 or 12 knots however, in so-called marginal planing conditions. At this point, it can pay to luff up 10 or 20 degrees towards the wind to promote planing.

Look around you in a race in marginal planing conditions, and you will see that there are many different angles and techniques for getting downwind at almost exactly the same speed. Some

Heeling to windward can help gain depth in light winds

techniques are more appropriate than others at different points in a race, depending on the tactical situation you are in.

In light airs, when planing is off the agenda, in some asymmetrics it can pay to ease the tack line a few inches, heel the boat over to windward and swing the gennaker to windward and away from behind the other sails. Now you are turning the gennaker into more of a conventional spinnaker. I can't tell you it will work in all boats, but it certainly works in the SB20, and other experts we interviewed said it worked in boats as diverse as the RS Feva and the Melges 24.

It pays to experiment and try lots of different ways of sailing downwind, because there is often no single right answer. Get comfortable with sailing high and fast, and low and slow because they are both important skills to have in your armoury.

For the rest of this chapter, we hand over to our experts who provide their own class-specific input as to what makes their kind of asymmetric boat go fast. Some of it you may find contradictory. Not all experts agree, for example, on whether or not to raise the centreboard downwind. So don't take their word as gospel. Use their tips as inspiration to do your own experimenting, and find out what works for you and your type of boat.

Expert Advice

Rick Perkins: Boat speed in high performance skiffs

Asymmetric Sailing: Going in a straight line, just going flat out fast in a Musto Skiff. How do you do it?

Rick: Well let's assume we're in a trapezing breeze, it's very much about feel and trim. Get yourself out on the trapeze, get your foot in the strap so you feel nice and stable and comfortable on the wire. Get your shoulders back into the harness. Make sure you're getting maximum leverage and then trim your mainsail in fairly close to the centreline of the boat so you're opening up the slot between the spinnaker and the mainsail and then just trimming the kite to find the sweet spot.

That sweet spot will vary depending on different classes, but I find that just I'm constantly easing to get the front of the asymmetric just lifting and then trimming back on. Ease the trim back on and just feel for when things are right. Keeping your body tilted back and just steering gently, keeping a nice neutral helm.

When it gets a bit lighter and you're not trapezing, then you've got the challenge of trying to decide which mode is going to be the quickest in terms of VMG. It can

(Continued)

Full pace in a Musto Skiff

be very tempting to sail a bit higher and see if you can get yourself out on the wire, but then you're going to be sailing a greater distance. So learn by looking at the other boats around you and experimenting perhaps outside of racing to try and find what are the best modes in different wind speeds for your particular class. It always surprises me how going fast tends to yield the best VMG. So if you're in a sort of transitional phase where you're not sure whether to get on a wire and sail a bit further, I generally find that higher and faster is the best option. If you've got a choice where you could sit on the side of the boat and soak low or you could head up a bit and sail a further distance out on the trapeze. Typically, I find that in the Musto Skiff, it's preferable to take the longer distance at the higher speed. But that's not going to be the case for every class . . .

Asymmetric Sailing: Yes, I would say in the SB20 the default safer option – if you're in doubt as to which mode to choose – is to soak, take the slower but shorter route . . .

Rick: Yes, I think the difference between a Musto Skiff when it's in displacement mode and when it's planing in terms of boat speed is enormous. You could perhaps go from like 6 knots to 12 knots or even more. So that's a huge difference in boat speed whereas perhaps with a keelboat the difference between going high and fast and low and slow in terms of absolute boat speed through the water is probably not so great. In the lighter boats I think the tendency would always be to try and search for the high-speed option.

Asymmetric Sailing: In terms of trimming the kite, is it always just have it on the curl?

Rick: Yes, the only time that I would deviate from that is if I'm wanting to slow the boat down because of a wave set or fear of crashing. So, typically, I'm trying to keep the kite on the curl, just like I would with a conventional spinnaker.

Asymmetric Sailing: And then from what you've just said, occasionally you'll overtrim the kite and use it as a brake. You'll slow yourself down intentionally?

Rick: Yes, if you're wanting to moderate speed because of a wave set or because you've got a port and starboard situation, oversheeting the kite is just like taking your foot off the gas.

Asymmetric Sailing: And then mainsail trim, how do you know when it's trimmed right?

Rick: If you've got the mainsail out too far the mainsail will effectively choke the slot between the two sails. A common mistake that new people in the Musto Skiff make is, they do their hoist and they get out on the wire, but they've forgot to trim the main on. So the boat is kind of less balanced because the main is out, it's slower because it's choking the slot. It's also because the head of the mainsail is a long way out, and so is pushing the bow down as well. It's much better for your straight line speed to pull the mainsail in. In terms of a reference, if the end of the boom is over the rear quarter of the hull, that's roughly where you need to be and you can trim the mainsail depending on how you're doing in terms of height.

So for instance, if you're wanting to, if you've understood the layline and you want to sail up a bit higher, you can ease a bit of mainsheet which will enable you to sail the boat higher to the wind with the mainsail eased. And, in extreme cases, if you're really wanting to try and make the mark, you can ease the main further. You have to beware that you can get your boat set up into quite an unstable state at that point – in that you can get yourself into almost an involuntary gybe. All of the power is in the spinnaker ahead of the mast and the mainsail's not really doing anything, so if you let the kite flog there's a danger of losing all the power in the rig and capsizing to windward.

Asymmetric Sailing: So there's something a little bit counterintuitive there for some people, when you talk about wanting to point up higher. If you want to

(Continued)

make a gybe mark or something you're actually easing the main whereas most of the time when you think about trying to get up higher you're thinking about pulling the mainsail in. But actually downwind with an asymmetric it's the opposite with the mainsail, is that right? If you want to go low you pull the mainsail in further?

Rick: Yes, as you sail higher the boat will power up. If you were sitting on the side you sail a bit higher so you can get on the wire, and if you sail higher the boat powers up even more. If you're desperately trying to make a buoy or a layline you can lose some of that power by dropping the mainsail off, but it does make the boat pretty unbalanced. One of the ways you can counteract that is to sail the boat heeled. Also, because you're going a little bit slower, the apparent wind comes further back. It's

Use the mainsheet as your height/depth control. Pull it in to sail deeper, ease it to sail higher

always important to have the mainsheet accessible when you're going in a straight line so you can trim it, especially for the lighter sailors. I suspect I trim my mainsail a little bit more than some of the heavier guys.

Asymmetric Sailing: What do you do with the centreboard downwind?

Rick: I never touch it. It goes in when we launch and it comes out when I come back. The only time I ever touch daggerboard is when it's really, really windy. I might raise it a few inches prior to the start and that's really to improve what's going on upwind. It takes the power out of the foils. I have seen people in very light winds trying to lift the centreboard or daggerboard to try and help them to soak even further downwind, but my experience is that it doesn't really make much difference. You tend to get all sorts of bits of string tangled around it, plus also because the boom is low you've got to fiddle around with it when you're gybing. So, on balance, I think it's a question of leave it down and forget about it.

Dave Hivey: Boatspeed in medium-performance hiking dinghies

Asymmetric Sailing: In the RS200 and RS400 fleets you're doing windward/leeward courses most of the time. So how do you achieve the best VMG?

Dave: First you've got to hot it up to get the speed in the first place. But once you go high, a lot of people then stay high. What you got to do is – once your apparent wind starts to shift forwards – then bring it down, trim your sails accordingly with that. This means your sails are actually overtrimmed to what they should be. I tend to get a really uneasy feeling around my stomach and the boat starts to feel a bit light when it starts to drop off the plane. And the easy thing to do then is just to shove the rudder, or to do nothing about it, and the boat drops right off the plane. You have to come all the way back up again and just try and get it planing again.

What you really should do in that situation when you're sat down is the crew and the helm move together if possible. But certainly me being the bigger bloke on most of the boats that I sail, is to drop the weight onto my toes, ease the mainsail a little bit, because my apparent wind has shifted. Then use the leeward heel of the boat

Dave Hivey and Mari Shepherd at full bore in the RS200

(Continued)

to bring it up to the wind ever so slightly to hold the boat planing – and then you can steer it back down again. If you do nothing initially, you've got to stop and start all over again. If you do that continually down the run, that will cost you a hundred metres by the bottom.

Asymmetric Sailing: And you said something that's probably counterintuitive there to most people – easing the main, when you might be thinking you actually need to sheet the mainsail in to keep the power on. Does it feel like the right thing to do?

Dave: No, not at all. It's a very, very strange thing to do and I don't think there are very many people that do it really. I only really got the hang of it fairly late in the RS200. That thing when the apparent wind starts to shift back again to ease the main and then to come back up again is, well, it's quite a weird thing to do really.

Asymmetric Sailing: It's more obvious with a gennaker. If you're trimming the gennaker at the time and you can sort of see what the wind is doing in relation to the curl of the gennaker, but with the mainsail it's quite hard to do that, isn't it?

Dave: It is. You can help yourself a little bit by having kind of a multitude of telltales going up the main. If you look at my mainsail, it looks a bit ridiculous actually, the

Large mainsail, small kite means more emphasis on correct mainsail trim in the RS200

If Dave Hivey was sailing his own RS200, this mainsail would have lots of telltales to help him set it correctly downwind

amount of telltales I've got on it. But it tends to help me with setting the mainsail. We set the lower telltales with the mainsheet and then you adjust the kicker to set the upper ones and you can use those telltales quite effectively. But they will also show you at that instant where the breeze drops off. You'll see them start to flutter and if you look at them quite often, it will actually give you good hints as to what to do.

Asymmetric Sailing: And that's the main reason for having those telltales stuck on the mainsail, is it?

Dave: Yes. My problem was I was always quite slow downwind. I was always very, very quick upwind and very slow downwind. So my nickname in the fleet was 'road blocker', I was that slow downwind. But I needed to spend a lot more time working on my downwind boat speed. And, in an asymmetric boat, it gets really difficult just to know where to set the mainsail. You can pull it in two or three feet sometimes and it doesn't seem to have any noticeable effect, although it does actually make a difference. And by having those telltales up and setting the low ones for your mainsheet and the upper ones for your kicker makes a big difference. On the RS200 the

(Continued)

kite isn't that big. It's not a masthead sail. So there's still quite a lot of drive being taken from the main and certainly a lot of drag being taken from the main if it's not in the right position.

Asymmetric Sailing: One of the other differences between a RS200 or 400 and most other asymmetrics is that they have pivoting centreboards rather than straight up-and-down daggerboards. So what do you do with the centreboard downwind?

Dave: I leave it all the way down unless it's very, very light. So if we're on real, real soaking mode and only in flat water. The challenge with the 200 is they're very twitchy, quite difficult to sail in soaking conditions to keep the boat dead, dead flat, or even slightly heeled to windward to float the kite round. But if you can do that *and* lift the centreboard up half way as well, you can gain some serious depth downwind. Robbie Burns is exceptionally good at doing that. I don't know how he keeps his boat that well balanced downwind. It's ridiculous with the centreboard almost all the way up but he gains so much depth downwind.

Use the jib as your 'burgee' to indicate how low you can sail in soaking mode

Asymmetric Sailing: So why doesn't everyone do it?

Dave: It's very tricky. You need to use very, very subtle body movements over every single wave and every single gust and if you don't do it well, it's worse than not doing it the first place. For the helm, unless you're very competent in moving your shoulders at exactly the right time, it's counter-productive, because the kite will collapse almost continuously. As soon as you start to get any chop or waves then it becomes very difficult to pull it off. Actually, the safest thing to do most of the time so you don't end up collapsing your kite, is to just leave the centreboard down.

Asymmetric Sailing: How low can you go when soaking in displacement mode, what's the limiting factor there?

Dave: In my opinion, the limiting factor is when the jib starts to drop back across – that's your limit. So, if you can take the boat as low as you can, have a slight bit of windward heel to float the kite around windward. The lowest point you can go is when the jib starts to drop back across to windward. In these conditions I like my crew to play the kite with one hand to hold the jib sheet in the other. If the jib starts to back, they give it a little flick back again straight away. As soon as the jib pops across, it kills the flow in the kite. So that's your limit, you're always fighting on that line really, but it's worth doing. You have to sail it that low, otherwise you sacrifice so much depth.

Darren Bundock: Boat speed in high performance catamarans

Light winds

Asymmetric Sailing: Darren, let's say we're sailing a Tornado or Formula 18, a high-performance multihull with trapeze. We want to get downwind on a VMG run as quickly as possible. Let's go through the wind range starting with light wind. Tell us about boat trim and sail trim. . .

Darren: Light wind is about going low and trying to soak as much as possible. You're not at a stage when you trying to fly a hull but you are trying to get some apparent wind across the sail. You're doing around 90 degree gybing angles and just keeping your apparent going but always just trying to soak as low as possible. That applies whether you're sailing with a gennaker or without. It's a trade-off between building the speed and then using the speed to get a little bit of depth. I guess that's where the skill comes in – judging your speed against your depth. It's about getting the best VMG out of the boat.

There isn't enough wind to get the windward hull out in just 4 knots of wind, but the centreboards are raised up a fair way. You still need a little bit of centreboard

(Continued)

Use crew weight to lift the windward hull as soon as possible

down – especially on the leeward hull to stop the boat from going sideways – so you can still build the apparent wind. But, as the wind builds, you need to keep more and more board down until you can get to a stage where you can fly a hull with the crew down the leeward side. That's when you need a lot more centreboard down to give the boat a bit more traction and something for the boat to work against, to help get the windward hull out of the water.

Asymmetric Sailing: Just getting back to the real light wind, with both hulls still in the water, how do I know if I'm soaking the right amount or when am I soaking too low? What are the tell-tale signs that I'm being too greedy and sailing too deep?

Darren: It's a balance between speed and depth, really. It's always good to judge boats around you as well. A lot of people use just the telltales flying off the bridle. Getting them flying at about 90 degrees is a good indication that you've got it pretty well right. That applies for a spinnaker boat and also an A-Class cat as well.

Asymmetric Sailing: What about boat trim in terms of where crew position is? Obviously you want to be far forwards, what about side to side?

Darren: In that very light stuff you want to get as much crew weight forward. Getting the transoms out of the water is nice, so you've got no 'bubbling' coming out of the transoms. You want to get as far forward. A lot of people will sit to leeward in that very light stuff but I really don't think it makes a difference whether you've got the weight stacked to windward or to leeward. I actually prefer to stack it to windward and get a little bit of a feel like if you're sailing a Laser by the lee where the mast is leaning over a bit to windward. That's my preferred technique but then you'll see a lot of the other good guys with the weight down to leeward. It's a personal thing, I suppose. It doesn't seem to make much difference, but I always feel that it's a little bit easier to catch the waves when the weight is stacked to windward, so that's why I prefer it.

Light-to-medium winds

Asymmetric Sailing: Now the wind is picking up a bit and you're close to lifting a hull. If there is an option to continue to soak with two hulls in the water, or a slim opportunity of lifting a hull, what are your choices now?

Darren: There is a crossover period, where there are gains or losses to be made, depending on whether you choose to go low or whether you choose to heat it up a little bit and try and pop that hull. I think if you're

Keep crew weight well forward in light winds

on a high-performance boat, I always go for popping a hull and getting the apparent wind going. The easiest way to encourage that is a little bit more centreboard down on the leeward hull, and you can actually start to trip the boat on that centreboard as well. So centreboard down and also, I always find in the lighter stuff it's more beneficial to actually fly the hull higher as well. This gives you a little bit of leeway [margin of error] because the hard bit is getting that windward hull out of the water and losing suction from the water surface. So, if you're up higher, you're getting more warning before it comes down and dips in the water again. It gives you a bit more reaction time and it also gets the weight of the mast helping you keep that hull up as well because the mast leaning away to leeward gives you some weight to work against.

Asymmetric Sailing: Nice tip! And then what about crew positioning?

Darren: You still want to have the weight a fair way forward but the critical thing is, you don't want any white water coming over the bow and on to the deck. If you

(Continued)

Flying the hull high in light airs means the weight of the mast gives you something to work against

Aim to lift the windward hull as soon as you think there is sufficient power to do so

start getting that then you're obviously too far forward and the hull is sticking into the waves and slowing you down rather than slicing through them.

Asymmetric Sailing: Is there ever any time when you go for the high mode a little bit too soon and other boats are soaking down inside you because they've stayed in a lower mode?

Darren: Oh yes, for sure. And I guess that's the toughest decision, when you can make big gains or losses, because if you go too early, and you're sailing too high and not going fast enough, you can lose a lot of ground very quickly. So there's definitely a crossover.

Asymmetric Sailing: Do you like to be the first to make that move? Or do you like other people to be the guinea pig?

Darren: It's about feeling the pressure. When you feel you've got a lot of pressure and you can pop up that hull easily then you go for it. But if you're struggling to pop that hull and you do it and you look around and you go a lot higher than everyone else then you know you can't afford to be doing it for too long. The key indicators are the boats around you, and using them as your gauge of what to do.

Medium winds

Asymmetric Sailing: Now, when the wind is picking up to the point where it's easy to fly the hull all the time, what are the little things that make the difference here?

Darren: Once you do have enough breeze where you are popping the hull easily, and your crew's moved up to the windward side and you're both sitting on the windward side, this is the easiest mode to sail in and people of all skill levels are very similar. But it's very important to make sure you've got the twist right in the mainsail. Generally, all the telltales are flying on your mainsail at this point, and your leech ribbons are starting to fly at the back. When you are just trying to pop that hull you are often just oversheeting a little bit to build up the low pressure on the leeward side of the sail to get that hull out. But once the hull is up, start feeding a bit of sheet when you get a gust. When you get a gust as you bear away, you can also let a handful of sheet out, as the boat bears away as well. This means that when the breeze dies and you start to come back up again to keep your apparent going, you've got an armful of mainsheet to pull in, to pull that hull back out again.

Asymmetric Sailing: Are you talking gennaker sheet, main sheet or both?

Darren: Both. If you get hit by a gust, you've always got to keep easing your gennaker out. It's very easy to oversheet the gennaker, and you really feel the boat accelerate

(Continued)

In medium and strong airs, ease the gennaker with every gust

when you can ease into a gust. Crew position is quite important as well. At this stage you are starting to move back as well, keeping that bow from starting to dig in or nosedive. You don't want any white water coming over the bow and so you should be moving back a little bit.

Asymmetric Sailing: Is there ever a time when you're VMG running to have both of you on the trapeze?

Darren: If you're right up on the layline and you think you're going to overlay – that's the only time we found on the Formula 18 and the Tornado that twin-trapezing has been beneficial. Sometimes it can help if you're catching waves and going over the top of them. But most of the time, no. Nearly always just the crew on trapeze, helm in the boat.

Strong winds

Asymmetric Sailing: Now, moving on to strong winds, what changes from the moderate breeze set-up?

Darren: The main thing is you can just pull that centreboard a bit more. The crew's out on trapeze starting to get right back and as soon as you get hit by a gust then you bear away, a good ease on the spinnaker, a little bit on the main as well so the boat

Even in strong winds the helm stays sitting rather than trapezing

can accelerate. You should always be testing the spinnaker. Just see if you can let it out again and just have that spinnaker curling around, popping back and forth. The helm is basically just steering so that when you get hit by a gust you're just bearing away with it. If the wind drops a bit lighter then you're just coming back up again and you're just keeping that hull out of the water and crew comfortably stretched out on trapeze.

Asymmetric Sailing: Now when it gets a little bit windier and wavier, and worried about burying that leeward bow. What are you doing to avoid a pitchpole?

Darren: At this stage the crew is right on the back corner of the boat. And that's when the good crew techniques come into play with the crew getting the weight back rather than the weight out. The helm is anticipating the gust and trying to bear away as you get hit by the gust. As soon as you get hit by the gust, you're bearing away quite dramatically. I still find, at this stage, it's best to keep the hull up. It gets to the point where it is safer to push the boat harder than it is to start going a little bit more conservative because when you've got too hot, or when you've got one hull out of the water and you do a nosedive, the boat will round up and come out of the wave again. But if you've got two hulls flat and you nosedive, that's when it really wants to trip over and that's when people get into a lot of trouble.

(Continued)

In strong winds the crew should get right on the back corner of the boat, leaning aft

MAST ROTATION

Darren: As we come around the top mark, we let the mast rotation go. It generally sits where it wants to sit. It's only in a very light breeze where you actually have to pull it around and lock it around so it is sitting at 90 degrees. Apart from those light conditions, it is very important to let your mast rotation out. This means your mast is bending on the soft surface rather than on the fore and aft plane. The fore and aft won't actually snap off, but if it's on the sideways surface, then it actually just flexes when you get hit by a gust.

TRAVELLER POSITION

Darren: Traveller is always centered except in the extreme stuff when you're trying to get a bit of height and you're trying to go high, that's when you start dropping it down. Apart from that, it's always centred with the mainsail twisted because there's a lot more breeze coming off the gennaker. So the bottom half of the sail needs to be more twisted than the top half.

Boat Speed in Sports Boats

Brian Hutchinson: The dynamics of kite and boat trim in a sportsboat like the Melges 24

Asymmetric Sailing: Tell us about some of the physical movements around the boat, some of the mechanics involved in sailing a fast sportsboat like the Melges 24 downwind. I think you've said before that the best kite trimmers have done some windsurfing. Tell us about that . . .

Brian: You can actually pick up a lot just by watching windsurfers. What windsurfers do is they try to avoid stall in the sails and in the skeg. They position the rig and the board and their weight and the sail to get the most acceleration while having side load. They're trying to optimise their vectors at all times. The manoeuvres and the reaction times are quicker on a sailboard than on any other boat. Like a catamaran is very slow because they're going much faster – the loads don't change as quickly on a catamaran because their apparent wind is a major factor whereas the sailboard is much lighter and you need to react right away.

On a sailboard, when the puff comes, you do not trim, you ease. You ease, you let the boom out, you position the rig and the board to get the most forward acceleration. And then, once you've got up to speed, you're planing, you generally head up a little

(Continued)

Everyone on the boat has to be tuned into boatspeed, not just the trimmer

When the puff comes: ease, accelerate, trim in

bit and rake back and trim a little bit more. But you don't ever want to overtrim the boom because that's just death. That pulls you sideways and it's not fast. And that is the same way you sail a kite on any boat. But on a light and responsive keelboat like a Melges 24 you sail it very much like a sailboard.

Good trimming is not just the trimmer talking to the helmsperson – it's somebody telling the trimmer when the wind is about to come and from what angle, and you have a countdown to the puff. So everybody on the boat is maybe trimming the boat to weather so as to take full advantage, get the kite over the boat in the right position. It's about aligning the vectors. It's much like skiing or mountain biking or ski racing. All these things are about aligning your centre of effort.

Let's say we're in about 10 to 14 knots of wind. A puff comes, it's about to hit you, what do you do? Initially the vectors are going to be aft, relative to the boat and the apparent wind, so you'll be easing the kite as you get the crew weight slightly to weather more, the mainsheet would possibly go out just a click and the helm would

In a breeze, get everyone OUT, then AFT

(Continued)

steer down just a click till you're up to speed, within a couple of seconds. Then you start dialing back up and, after the kite has been eased, you start trimming it back in. The crew weight is positioned so that you have a feel for that dot where the centre of effort is on the sail. Everyone's focused on where they want to be – whether forward or aft or whatever it may be.

Asymmetric Sailing: OK, so you just explained what you should be doing. But what do you see other sailors and other teams doing that that they shouldn't be doing?

Brian: Mainly it starts with the trimmer, and the crew not recognising the effect they have on the kite. If you're in marginal conditions where the kite is barely flying or the leech wants to fall into the mainsail, there are certain things that you can do with the crew positioning, like get on the bow, get two people on the bow, to get the kite away from the main, maybe position the boat slightly to weather, or with the mast plumb upright in marginal conditions.

In heavy air, people think that you only want to be aft. At the beginning of the puff you want to be *out*, and as the puff matures, then you want to be *aft*. And you can't be walking around the boat that much if it's going 25 knots. You're basically back, you certainly want to concentrate your efforts outwards to help the boat bear away, much like you would rock the rig to weather on a sailboard to get the bow down. I think what I'm not seeing, is a total focus from the whole crew. Get everyone in the team focused on boat and sail trim, and you will be faster.

CHAPTER 8

RACING: TACTICS AND STRATEGY

Getting Around the Course

In high-performance boats that are difficult to sail well, it's vital to have good boathandling. Until you have reached a reasonable level of control over your boat, it's hard to apply tactics and strategy to your game plan on the race course. If you're still struggling to stay upright on basic manoeuvres such as tacking and gybing – and, believe me, I've been there with the 49er and Musto Skiff – then your game plan is to execute as few manoeuvres as possible. Maybe even start on port tack behind the fleet so that you can one-tack the first beat, go for a straight hoist (no gybe-set yet), slightly overstand the layline for the leeward gate so you know you can make it in one gybe. Then one-tack the next beat, and so on.

Even some of the best sailors pursue this strategy of simplicity. As they say: 'Keep It Simple Stupid!' And the KISS approach can work very well in fast asymmetrics where mistakes are so easy to make.

But let's assume that you've got a level of boathandling that will at least get you around the course in light-to-medium airs in pretty good order. The heavy-air finesse can come later.

Tactics v strategy

It can be easy to confuse tactics with strategy, so for the sake of clarity here are some definitions. At least, they're *my* definitions!

Good tactics help you execute your race strategy

- **Strategy** is the big picture, your pre-start plan. It involves looking at the effects on the race course such as any current, land effects, the prevailing wind, the weather forecast for the period of the race and so on. Before the start you should have a sense of what your strategy will be for sailing around the race track as fast as possible.
- **Tactics** is how you interact with the other boats on the race course. You want to be able to execute your strategy as closely as possible to your original plan, but other boats get in the way of that plan, especially if their strategy is similar to yours (which it often is!). So tactics are the short-term decisions that you make in order to negotiate your way as smoothly as possible around your rivals on the race course.

Getting the balance right between strategy and tactics is one of the great skills of competitive sailing. Let's say you're heading into the final race of a championship and it's down to you and another boat *Rival*. All you need to do is finish within five places of *Rival*. If there is stronger current heading upwind on the left-hand side of the course, but *Rival* tacks off to the right, which way do you go? Broadly speaking, strategy says go left for the favourable current, tactics says go right to cover *Rival*. Which is the right answer? Well, we probably don't have enough information to make that decision, but the important thing is to understand the difference between the demands of strategy and tactics.

Strategy and tactics for asymmetrics

The faster a boat travels through the water, the more expensive each manoeuvre becomes. A fast skiff like a 49er, and most multihulls, slow to a fraction of their speed through a tack. A slow boat like a Laser, on the other hand, loses barely any speed through a tack (at least not the way the Olympic sailors tack a Laser), so the price of each manoeuvre is much less expensive.

Boats lose less speed gybing, although in steady breezes you still want to keep your gybes to a minimum.

The better your boathandling, the wider your tactical options

So can you start to see the importance of what we said earlier about having good boathandling skills? The better and faster you can execute your basic manoeuvres, the more you can afford to make, and the more strategic and tactical decisions become available to you.

Let's start looking at some of the factors that feed into your strategic and tactical game plan, and how they will affect your decision making.

Gusts are king

As mentioned earlier, the way that an asymmetric gennaker works is by harnessing the power of apparent wind. We have also learned how important it is to find the strongest wind to create the most efficient airflow across your gennaker. With that in mind, you must remember that, above all else, gusts are king. Looking for dark water when you're sailing downwind is vital in any form of sailboat racing, but in high-performance asymmetric boats, it is almost without exception the most important thing that you can do.

The difference between finding that extra gust of 2 or 3 knots of breeze on one side of the course compared with your competitors in slightly less breeze, can result in hundreds of metres gain in a very short time. So, one of the keys is to look over your shoulder, but not as far behind you as you would on most conventional boats. Growing up in slow boats, most of us have learned to look over our rear shoulder, past the transom to see where the next puffs of wind

Looking for the strongest breeze should be your top priority

are going to reach the boat. But if your boatspeed is close to true wind speed, then you need to change your perspective.

In fast asymmetrics, now that we're sailing across the wind and we're also sailing much faster in relation to the wind speed, we need to be looking over our forward shoulder and seeing where the wind is going to reach us from a beam of the boat, rather than behind us.

In extreme cases, where you're sailing very high-performance asymmetrics and you're even exceeding true wind speed, then you actually need to be looking forward of the beam, maybe 45 degrees to windward of the bow, much as you might do when you're look-ing for gusts upwind. It's quite possible that the gust you encounter at the top of the

When boatspeed exceeds wind speed, you need to be looking forward of the beam for the next gust

windward leg, you could then meet a second time on the way downwind as you overtake the same gust!

When you're moving into asymmetrics from slower boats, it can take a lot of experience to get a sense of when the gust is going to hit, but certainly, the most important thing is to understand the wind is going to reach you from a lot further forwards than you're used to. It might also mean that you find the wind or the gusts take a lot longer to reach you than you expect, because you're sailing away from the gusts coming up behind you. In fact in super-fast multihulls such as the America's Cup AC45, it's quite possible that they will encounter a gust on their way upwind to the windward mark, hoist the gennaker and then catch up with the very same gust downwind as they travel at two or three times true wind speed!

STAYING IN THE GUST

If the wind is gusting in streaks, rather than uniformly across the course, it pays to get into the stronger streak and stay in it as long as possible. If you can see a gust out to one side of you, arc the boat up and sail faster towards it. Once you are in the gust, bear away and soak a little more so that you stay in the gust as long as possible. And even gybe if you think that will keep you sailing in the gust for longer.

Expert Advice

Chris Nicholson: Looking for the wind

My general impression is that a lot of skiff sailors look too far behind them. In a 49er or an 18-foot skiff, my angle of focus would be about 45 degrees to windward of the bow. Look much further behind you than that, and the breeze you're looking at may never reach you. Basically, the faster your boat, the further forward you need to be looking to see the breeze that will affect you.

I also look to leeward in a fairly wide arc to see what breeze I can expect to pick up when I gybe. I don't find it too easy to work out the breeze I'm going to be in when I've gybed, so this is why my point of focus is wider. But I think in a 49er you should be looking out beyond the aft quarter for an idea of what to expect after the gybe.

Look over your front shoulder for the next breeze

You want to look for the darkest water and aim to pick that breeze up. If you can see lighter water ahead and to windward, then you need to be looking over your shoulder to see if you'll be getting more wind if you gybe. In bright sunlight, when the sun can make it quite hard to pick out the strength and direction of the breeze, I use polarised sunglasses as these really help bring out the contrast in dark and light on the water.

It can pay to swing a little higher on the trapeze to help you look around more easily at what's going on. I'd guess I spend around 30 to 40 per cent of my time looking around. 49ers are difficult to make sure they're going at 100 per cent pace all the time, but it's worth sacrificing a bit of all-out speed to keep an eye on the bigger picture.

Finding the strongest breeze remains the priority until the boat is going really fast in strong wind. Then, angle of breeze gets more important. Knowing how to weigh up the relative merits of gusts and shifts is really down to experience.

(Continued)

Rick Perkins: Sailing in clear air is fast

Sailing in clear air is fast. It's an obvious statement, but it's crucial to bear it in mind when sailing asymmetrics downwind.

Because wind pressure makes such a difference to boatspeed, and because you have such a narrow angle for achieving optimum speed, it's worth carving yourself a lane where you can sail the boat how you want to sail it. Sailing in a big fleet, sailing in the pack, is pretty slow compared to just having a bit of free space and doing your own thing. That's why the gybe-set often works out well for people, because they have the space to do their own thing over on the left-hand side whereas the bulk of the fleet tends to go to the right. People can often make up good ground, not because it was the correct side of the run to go, but because they've just been sailing the natural fast angles. Where everyone else has been sailing non-optimum angles defending their lane, those sailing in clear air are getting top speed out of their boats.

Sailing in clear air is faster than sailing in company, so try to make some space for yourself

The Windward Mark

Start looking for the gust early

So, if we're going to find the darkest water to get the strongest gust, then we need to start planning how we're going to catch that first gust from well before we reach the windward mark. Start looking upwind and look at the water to windward of the windward mark. Make a decision where you think the strongest wind is going to be and what manoeuvre is going to take you most quickly to that dark line of breeze. As you look upwind, if it's to the left of the windward mark, then a straight set should do it nicely; just bear away, hoist, and sail into that gust. But if, as you look upwind, the best darkest breeze looks like it's on the right, then not only might you experience a little bit of that gust as you approach the windward mark, but the quickest way to harness that gust once you've hoisted the gennaker is by executing a gybe-set manoeuvre.

Plan your downwind leg well before you get to the windward mark

LIFT OR HEADER?

One of the other tell-tale signs to look out for as you're approaching the windward mark is whether you're on a header or a lift as you approach the mark. If you're on your final starboard approach to the mark and you find yourself being lifted above the layline, then a lift on starboard would mean that you would want to gybe-set so that you get that same change in wind direction, creating a header on port gybe. Remember that just as you want to make the most of the lifts on the windward leg, you want to make the most of the headers on the downwind leg, because it's the headers that take you closer to the leeward mark. If, on the other hand, you find yourself being headed as you approach the windward mark and you're struggling to even get around the windward mark, then this is a tell-tale sign that opting for a straight hoist and remaining on starboard gybe would be a good thing.

Getting into position at the windward mark

Another factor to consider in your tactics is your positioning relative to the rest of the fleet. Remember that your primary goal is to get into the strongest wind. So for example, if you

Where you tack on the layline will determine where you can sail down the run

encounter good strong wind up the right hand side of the course as you approach the windward mark, then you know that you want to be gybe setting to be able to capture that new wind really early on the downwind leg. This means you want to be in position to complete the gybe-set without fouling other boats. So plan ahead and start booking your space for an inside rounding at the windward mark.

If you've been approaching the layline from quite high and other boats are running into you on their approach to the layline, then you have some work to do here. Rather than racing to try to get over the top of the boats just to leeward of you, it might pay to slow down, let them go and create a space in the line around the windward mark. This will mean that you are clear to gybe immediately as you pass the windmark and get into that strong tactical gybe-set position.

On the other hand if the best breeze is to be found by doing a straightforward bear-away then you will need to negotiate the majority of the fleet also setting their gennakers on starboard. Now there are other considerations. Largely what you do next is determined by how long you have until you need to gybe. If you are on a short course and you are expecting to gybe in the next two or three minutes then you want to make sure that you are in a position to be able to do that gybe when you choose to. It may not pay you to pull off a fast efficient hoist and get up on the windward hip of another boat unless you can get up and around the front of him in time for your gybe.

Instead, it may be better to hold fire on your fastest hoist and aim to dive down low to match the line of that boat in front. Even better if you can dive lower to leeward of his line – because this puts you in the controlling position to be able to gybe when you want.

When should I gybe-set?

Most of the time, the straight set is the safest tactical call, particularly at the first windward mark when there's a lot of traffic. Also, from a boathandling perspective, gybe-setting is a tricky manoeuvre to get right. But there can be great tactical reasons for giving it a go. Here are five factors that might tempt you to make that early gybe.

More wind

By now you should already understand the importance of stronger wind when you're sailing dynamic and responsive asymmetric boats. Of course, if the wind is blowing really hard, then staying upright is the priority and pulling off a gybe-set can be a tricky manoeuvre. So you have to balance your tactical considerations against your boathandling ability. Better to hoist, set, then gybe when you're up to full pace if you're worried about falling in.

More wind is the best reason to gybe early

Wind shifts

Hooking into an extra 3 or 5 knots of breeze is by far the most important considera-tion in an asymmetric boat, but if the wind strength is even across the course, think next about wind shifts. If you are approaching the windward mark on a nice starboard lift, you will want to gybe to take advantage of the same shift, which once you're going down-wind will be a port header. If a header up the end of the beat made it hard to make the windward mark on starboard tack, that is your cue to go for a straight set and hoist the gennaker on starboard.

If you pick up a starboard lift which is also gusting, then you will most likely want to gybe straightaway. Your angles can change massively in this scenario, and you may find that you are almost pointing at the leeward mark once you have gybed. If you carry on and hoist onto starboard in this lifting gust situation, you are in danger of overstanding the layline and losing ground to those who gybe-set behind you.

Tidal considerations

If there is current or tide on the course, then remember that what helps you upwind hinders you downwind, and vice versa. So be aware of the state of the tide around each mark and consider your tactics accordingly.

Where is the fleet?

We've thought about some strategic factors, now let's think about some tactical, boat-to-boat considerations. If you're rounding the windward mark for the first time, in the front half of the fleet, chances are there'll be a line of boats behind you on the starboard layline. This creates a big wind shadow in the area just to leeward, so you have to have a really good case for gybe-setting in this situation. If you've just been enjoying that big starboard lifting gust we talked about earlier, then go for that gybe-set, and you'll soon be out of that nasty wind hole. Short-term pain for long-term gain. Otherwise, hoist on starboard and sail for at least 100 metres before making your first gybe. That way, you'll avoid the worst of the disturbed air. But if you're in the back half of the fleet, the wind hole won't be so great, so you can revert to your strategic priorities.

If you're close to the back of the fleet, gybe-setting offers a good roll of the dice

Nothing to lose

If you're right at the back and running out of time to make up places in the race, then your best bet is often to do the opposite to what most of the fleet is doing. As at least three-quarters of the fleet usually does a straight hoist on starboard, you have nothing to lose in gybe-setting and seeing if you pick up a 'gust from heaven' on the left hand side of the course. You've really got nothing to lose in this situation, because unless a load of boats capsize, you're unlikely to overtake them going the same way. Might as well gybe and roll the dice for a bit of luck!

Expert Advice

Steve Irish: Get on to the 'long gybe'

Most of the time you will find the majority of the fleet will do a straight set on starboard, because the gybe-set's quite a risky manoeuvre. So then your consideration is: which is your 'long gybe'? In other words, which gybe you will be on for longer? If the long gybe is starboard then you might go for the roll or stay higher or just hold your lane. You need to maintain clear air as long as possible. If it's actually long gybe port then you're going to be looking for a soak, so the set needs to be low. This will give you control over your point of gybe, to set you up for clear air on the long gybe.

Seizing Your Opportunities

Geoff Carveth looks back at a crucial decision point in a world championship

Going into the final race of the 2008 SB20 Worlds in Ireland, Geoff Carveth found himself in a three-way battle for the championship title. Rounding the windward mark in 33rd place was not the kind of race he needed. Time for desperate – but calculated – measures.

'We sailed high to get over the fleet initially. Our decision was not to go deep anyway, for tactical reasons. We definitely wanted to be in charge of our own destiny. There was no need to gybe basically, so we wanted to be going over boats rather than creeping down low and having no options to hot up. So we hoisted and sailed high just to get over the first batch of boats. As we did so, we thought maybe there was enough breeze to go for a hotter angle. The whole fleet in front of us was sailing in a deep, soaking mode.

'As we hotted up to go over maybe one or two boats, we thought maybe there was enough wind to get planing. Also, the right hand side of the course looked darker on the water and possibly windier, so we said "let's go for it." The boatspeed jumped from

Geoff Carveth and crew winning the 2011 SB20 Worlds

about 7 or 8 knots to maybe 12 or 13, and we were locked in and going fast. If the wind had died we would have been in trouble, but it stayed solid. And at least we were in clear air. We could see everyone else was slowing each other down further to leeward.

'We gybed right in the corner of the course, far away from anyone else. But the breeze held for us and with the apparent wind we were generating we were coming back into the leeward gate with good pace, underneath all the boats trying to soak down. We had climbed up to 6th or 7th by the bottom, enough to put us in a commanding position for the championship. Stupidly, we did the same thing again down the next run, but it worked again, and we were up to 1st in the race. And so we won the Worlds.'

Roll, Don't Be Rolled!

Melges 24 World Champion Brian Hutchinson talks about the importance of holding your nerve and your course when you're jostling for position down the run. . .

Asymmetric Sailing: How should you work the boat when you're in a tight situation with other boats around you, maybe trying to roll you?

Brian: Well, at the 2011 Worlds we rolled some really good boats and it was a problem that they had with the alignment of the forces going through the boat – of the centre of effort and the sails and the stalling of the foil underwater. What was happening was that we would come up on the weather hip of the boat, and you would see they were starting to get nervous

Work hard to roll other boats if the paying gybe is to continue on starboard

and they would send the boat up. The bow goes up to try to prevent being rolled, but that immediately just slows you down. The helmsman often tries to react by putting the bow up – and so the punishment is more severe, and earlier. So we would roll them because we're already coming at them at an optimum angle. We don't react, we are already in a roll position and if it's near the layline it's even better because you pulled them out of their optimum heading. Then you roll right into a gybe ahead of them, and: Boom! Got 'em! It happens all the time on boats with asymmetric kites. Get that boat ahead of you to sail out of their optimum angle and then you have them.

Asymmetric Sailing: Now, in that case, if you had been the other boat that was ahead and to leeward, what would you have done?

Brian: Well, if I'm on sheet not calling tactics, it's really unnerving to have that scenario even happen because the person calling upwind and tactical conditions should warn us that there is a boat coming which could affect us at some point. Now before that happens, if I were the boat ahead, I would either already be ready to go into a gybe and sucker them into trying to roll and go high mode just before gybing. Otherwise, I would just concentrate on going fast to make sure we are maybe in a fast mode versus a depth mode. With these boats, you really

Don't allow an attacking boat to drag you too far off your ideal VMG course

have to look at the conditions. If it's a choppy condition, chances are that you want to be in a depth mode, not in a high mode. This is because you're probably going to make greater gains by just sailing at medium deep mode and maintaining a constant pressure, never losing pressure on each wave. So if you can maintain constant pressure, you'll keep charging forward. So, if these guys want to roll you, fine. When it gets to the point you really have them leveraged, they really want to roll you – then just roll into a gybe, no big deal. But if they are coming at you from your leeward hip – then you've got a real problem because then they 'own' you already. Then when you gybe you have to really send it and try to get clear air. That's the situation you really want to avoid.

Judging Laylines

Judging laylines in an asymmetric boat can be very tricky, especially if the wind is unstable, because you would have already discovered just how much variations in wind strength and wind direction can affect the direction of your boat.

Laylines can move around with every gust and lull

If it is lighter winds, then it may pay to overstand the layline. This means you keep lots of apparent wind running over the sails as you approach the leeward mark, and anybody who is coming in a little bit too high and a little bit too deep will pay a high price with vastly reduced boatspeed. Remember, gennakers are hugely efficient sails, but only when they have flow across the sail. Coming in too high in light winds will kill your boatspeed.

So make sure that you are not one of those boats trying to run too deep with a limp gennaker. Make sure that you are one of the ones coming in hotted up and with lots of speed coming into that leeward mark, because your apparent wind will carry you through the dirty air of the slow boats to windward.

If you do find that you are coming into a leeward mark a little too high and you are starting to run deep, look around you, and make a decision about whether you should cut your losses early and put in two more gybes to get down to the mark. In light winds, the loss of distance from two gybes is minimal, and the boathandling is relatively straightforward. More often than not it's better to go for the double gybe than blob along with a floppy gennaker.

In stronger winds, this is a bigger decision because you lose more distance through a gybe compared with your straight line speed. Not only that, there's also the risk of capsizing. So you really have to make this decision based on your confidence and your ability to gybe effectively.

With that in mind, we've already said that generally in light winds it pays to overstand the gybe mark in light airs. The same is often true in strong airs because, rather than facing the two extra gybes and the risk of broaching or capsizing, it is sometimes better to overstand the layline. It might mean that you have to drop the gennaker earlier and do some two-sail reaching to get back up to the leeward mark. But that may be a price worth paying compared with the risk of those two extra gybes and a resulting possible capsize.

Are you starting to see how the quality of your boathandling affects the quality of your tactical decisions?

Tidal considerations

These differ very little from those in other conventional spinnakered boats, except that the potential for gain or loss in, say, a strong tidal situation is much greater. This is because your separation across the course from one side to the other is much larger than on boats

In light winds, current becomes a crucial factor as you approach the leeward end of the course

with spinnaker poles that tend to stick to the rhumb line. If you are going down the run with the tide running with you, you can afford to gybe early even if you find yourself soaking to the mark, as the tide will carry you there. Far better to do that than gybe late and find you're having to tight-reach back to the mark as the tide tries to sweep you off downwind.

On the other hand, with the tide running against you down the run, you are safer to overstand on your final gybe, and come in towards the leeward mark with pace and control. There's nothing worse than running deeper and deeper towards the leeward mark against an adverse tide. The more you bear away the less efficient the gennaker becomes, and you often see people wrapping themselves around the leeward mark as a result. And that can ruin your day.

LEEWARD MARK APPROACH

On a normal port-rounding course, all other things being equal, aim to approach the leeward mark on starboard gybe. This gives you rights on other boats on pretty much every count. Outside of the three boatlengths circle, and you hold precedence on the basic port/starboard rule, and inside the three boatlengths you have water on boats outside of you.

Expert Tip

Chris Nicholson: When to gybe for the layline

Obviously, as you approach the layline, your time for gybing is running out. In most conditions I like to try to gybe a little bit early of the layline so that I can still get back to the centre of the course. In light winds you can sometimes get away with overstanding a little bit, as other boats above you try to soak too low to get to the mark. But be careful. Take a careful check of the pressure across the course before making this crucial gybe.

In strong winds, bear in mind it could take some time to get the gybe in safely, especially if there's a big seaway, so aim to get your gybe in earlier than you might think. When it's windy, don't be too sad if one or two boats roll you, just so long as you keep on moving – and stay upright!

Getting Through the Leeward Gate

The leeward rounding in short-course asymmetric racing is one of the most crucial parts of the race. If you're in the front pack, you need to think ahead and defend your position around

Keeping moving is the key to escaping the leeward gate

the mark. If you're behind, this is your main opportunity in the race to attack and get back into the leading pack.

We spoke to Chris Draper, Olympic medallist and double World Champion in the 49er, about his approach to this crucial phase of the race. He's talking about a leeward gate, although most of the same principles apply with a single leeward mark.

Chris Draper: The leeward gate

Keep on moving

The overriding factor with the leeward rounding is to get in and out of that area as fast as possible because it's such a stopping point. It's the only time in the race where boats really tend to slow down, so you want to minimise your 'down time'.

I think there's a good analogy here with when you're driving on the road and you want to overtake a car on a single-lane carriageway. You want to sit a little distance back from them, so that when your overtaking opportunity arrives you can use run-up speed to get past them, and spend the minimum time on the opposite side of the road. It's similar with the leeward mark; the more speed you come in with on your approach, the better the chance you have of getting out of there quickly too.

Think ahead

Because the leeward rounding is so important, in some cases we'll start to think about it even before we've rounded the windward mark. Normally, we'll sail past the gate at the start to check if there is any heavy bias, and we'll make a mental note about which one is favoured. Also, if we think one side of the course is favoured we'll make a plan to round the mark that takes us out to that side.

If we want the left hand mark (looking downwind), we might even think about a gybe-set at the windward mark. We've got a number of processes we'll go through when making our plan. But that plan could change depending on whether we're in attacking mode (i.e. looking to gain places) or defending mode (already in a top position).

If we're defending, we'll aim to make a fast windward mark rounding and to get to the leeward gate as quickly as possible. This might sound obvious, but this gets much harder when you're attacking, when there are many more things to think about.

Think ahead before the decision is made for you

When you've got space around you, and the luxury of selecting either leeward mark, you want to take the one that will get you out to what you expect will be the favoured side of the next windward leg. This means looking back upwind before your drop the gennaker, to see if there are any useful puffs or shifts coming down either side of the course.

Traffic avoidance

However, once you've got other boats to contend with, which more often than not you do, then your priorities can change dramatically. If you've got a lot of traffic queuing up to go around one mark, then it can pay to go around the other one even when it's further to sail there. Remember your No. 1 rule of getting in and out of this area ASAP.

If we're in attacking mode and wanting to come into the mark fast, we'll aim to come in tight on the layline with speed, and with rights at the mark, and usually aim for a gybe-drop inside the boats that are queuing up there. Remember that in an asymmetric boat, which sails wide angles downwind, you can establish rights on other boats sometimes from hundreds of metres away, because you're overlapped the whole way down.

If the bulk of the fleet around is aiming for one mark, it might pay you to sail further to the other mark just to stay in clearer air

But bear in mind that if you're aiming for a gybe-drop inside other boats, your boat handling had better be good. The better your boat handling, the more aggressively you can deal with the leeward mark situation. Good boat control gives you more tactical options.

Make sure that you plan well ahead. You can see plenty of people who only make their minds up about which leeward mark at the very last minute, but we do everything we can to avoid this. We rarely change our minds into the leeward gate; we'll discuss it a long way out and try very hard to avoid a situation where you have to make a spontaneous decision. Far better to make a solid plan than to be dictated to by other people, simply because you failed to think ahead.

Going for the favoured side

If you know that one side of the beat is favoured, and everyone else does too, then you know you've got a fight on your hands to get round the favoured leeward mark – unless of course you're in the lead. If we're quite forward in the fleet, and just looking to pick off the odd

If you've got a strong feeling one side of the beat is favoured, base your leeward gate strategy around that

boat or two, we might accept going around the favoured mark and hanging on to the same line as the leaders out of the mark.

But if we are looking to make big gains (i.e. we're further back in the fleet), then it might be worth taking the wrong leeward mark and then putting in an early tack over to the favoured side. This way, you'll have your own lane across to the favoured side. In a fast skiff like a 49er when you sail faster you go higher too, so you have the opportunity to sail past boats that are just 'chopping wood' [Draper-speak for boats that are pinching up and going slow as they see-saw through the waves].

However, if you have only got one boat in the queue ahead of your round the favoured mark, it can pay to foot out low from the leeward mark and grab some clean air ahead and to leeward. Of course, if there are other boats further ahead, then this isn't so good because you'll be gasping for air.

When you're racing to establish three-boatlengths rights with another boat, it can pay to hang on late to the kite, just so you get around in front of your rival. The crew can finish off the kite drop once you've rounded the mark with your nose in front. But, again, get out of there as quick as you can, and leave any non-vital tidying until you're fully sorted and up to speed away from the mark.

Judging laylines

Judging laylines in asymmetric boats can be tricky, but the biggest priority here is to make sure you're approaching the leeward mark at speed. You don't want to sail slow, and we'll avoid

Thinking ahead is the key to success, when trying to break through the log jam at the leeward gate.

soaking to the mark in all situations except for the very lightest of breezes, say 2–3 knots or less, because the drop in boatspeed is proportionally much less significant.

If it's windy, I'll look back up the middle of the course to see what pressure is coming when we gybe, and use that to gauge my most likely layline. Once we've gybed, my crew will take a transit on the mark and tell me how we're doing on it. His feedback will dictate how I steer to the mark. If it's very windy, we'll tend not to put in a gybe-drop, because that would be a very high-risk option that we'd rather avoid.

We've talked about what you should do, but just to emphasise some critical points, here is a quick list of don'ts:

Don't

- Soak to the mark – do an extra gybe instead (or get your layline right in the first place!).
- Think too late – make an early decision.
- Get stuck on the outside of a mark rounding – make sure you've got rights at the mark.

CHAPTER 9

THE RACING RULES

SAF's Racing Rules of Sailing have been around for a long time, and have been written primarily with slower boats in mind, which tend to sail directly from A to B.

Because the new breed of high performance boats with asymmetric gennakers travel faster and gybe through wider angles downwind, this makes it important to understand some of the implications when you bring the Racing Rules into the equation.

One of the nice aspects of fast asymmetric boats is that kinetics such as pumping, ooching and rocking tend not to have much of an effect on boat speed. In fact it's more likely you'll disturb the air flow over the sails and slow the boat down, so the dreaded Rule 42 tends not to have much relevance, with the possible exception of slower keelboats where kinetics can still have a small effect. Competing at a SB20 World Championship, I have seen overzealous umpires in action, so you still need to be careful. In any case, because the potential gains for artificial propulsion are so limited, it's really not worth testing the limits of Rule 42.

For this section of the book we have brought in Chris Simon, a skilled international judge with wide experience of racing at all levels of the sport, from the Volvo Ocean Race to Olympic competition to club racing.

Know Your Lefts From Your Rights

When you're looking at two gate marks, which do you call the left mark and which the right? It might sound like a stupid question, but there are two ways of looking at them and, if you're sailing on a boat with two or more people, then it's critical that everyone has the same understanding about which is left and which is right. When you're looking at a map of the course on shore in a race briefing, for example, it's fairly obvious which is left and which is right. Isn't it? Trouble is, when you're two minutes away from the leeward gate on a busy race course, when you, as the tactician, call for your team on the bow to get ready for a gennaker drop around the right-hand mark, exactly which one do you mean now? You might know what you mean, but do your team mates? On a team boat, you must have your terminology and communication absolutely straight. For the purposes of our conversation with Chris Simon, Chris suggested that we call it as we see it while sailing downwind on the race course. So as we're sailing downwind, the mark we see on the left is the 'left' mark and the one on the right is the 'right'. Right? Good. Now we can begin.

Leeward Gates

Asymmetric Sailing: The rules that govern your entry into the leeward gate zone can be very complicated, especially if the two marks are close together. . .

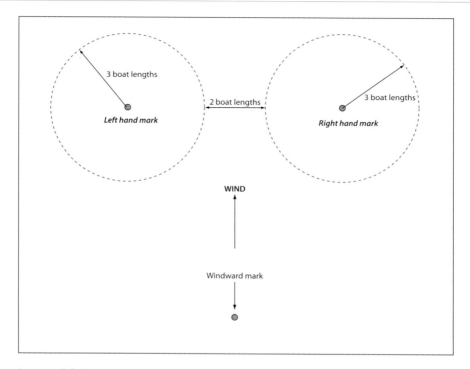

3 boat lengths

Left hand mark

2 boat lengths

3 boat lengths

Right hand mark

WIND

Windward mark

Leeward Gate

Chris: Under the old regime of a two boat-length zone, the recommendation for race management was that a gate should be six boat lengths in width. With the change of the standard zone to a three-length zone, race management recommendation has now changed so that the recommended separation is now eight boat lengths. So the aim is to have a two-boat-length space in the middle which is outside the zone of either mark. A problem arises if race committees lay the marks less than six lengths apart, in which case you have a sector in the middle where a boat could actually be in the zone of both marks. This can create potential rules issues, but provided the gate is set at the recommended space then, essentially, each mark can be looked at separately.

Collision course at leeward gate

Asymmetric Sailing: OK, so let's say there are two boats on different gybes on a collision course as they're approaching the leeward gate. One boat is coming in from the right-hand side and

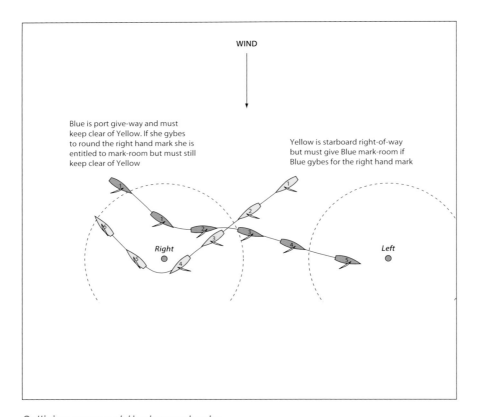

Collision course at the leeward gate

is wanting to go round the left-hand gate, so that boat would be on port gybe; then there is another boat on starboard gybe wanting to go round the right-hand mark. Talk us through the scenario.

Chris: As they approach the gate, provided both boats are outside the zone, it is just a straight port and starboard. There is no other complication until one of them reaches the zone of a mark.

Asymmetric Sailing: OK, so once the port-gybe boat enters the zone of the right-hand leeward mark, then it has rights to water at that mark. But what if for tactical reasons – say a lot of traffic and congestion at the right-hand mark – the port-gybe boat wanted to keep on heading over to the other mark on the left?

Chris: You have to make certain assumptions, and the assumption you must make is that a boat that enters the zone of a mark is treated as if it was going to round *that* mark. Quite frankly the other boat can't be expected to mind read. So if the boat on port comes into the zone of the right-hand mark, whether or not the starboard boat is at that time in the zone, the port-gybe boat is the inside boat and is entitled to mark room. The fact that they're on opposite gybes doesn't matter because the rule was changed so that boats sailing downwind on opposite gybes are overlapped.

Asymmetric Sailing: So the yellow boat at the moment thinks that the blue boat is going to gybe and round inside him. . .

Chris: In relation to the right-hand mark, yellow is faced with an inside boat within the zone and has therefore got to give that boat mark room. Now the port-gybe boat must give way because the normal right-of-way rule still applies, so she is a boat on port who's got to keep clear of the boat on starboard but the starboard boat has got to give mark room to the port boat. Mark room is room to sail to the mark, and I can think of one ISAF case in particular which says 'to the mark' means that she must sail within a 'corridor' that goes from the place where she entered the zone to the position where she would begin to alter course to round the mark. Provided she is within that corridor, she is protected because Rule 18.5 says that as long as she is taking mark room to which she is entitled, she can't be penalised for breaking another rule, in this case Rule 10, the port-starboard rule.

So the port tack boat has got a bit of a conundrum because she actually wants to round the left-hand mark. In order to do that she has got to give way to the starboard boat, because she will not be sailing to the right-hand mark. So her protection or exoneration from breaking the port-starboard rule would not apply if she just simply sailed straight through the zone of the right-hand mark going to the left-hand mark. The starboard boat has a clear-cut situation here, as the port boat has got to keep clear of her but she must give her mark room. If the starboard boat sees the port tack boat leave the corridor, in other words the port tack boat hardens up and points at the left-hand mark, then the starboard boat is entitled to shout 'Starboard!' and to expect her to keep clear.

Asymmetric Sailing: Is 'the corridor' a term that you would use in a protest scenario? Is it a recognised term?

Chris: Yes, I think it is. If you look at Case No.75 in the *ISAF Case Book*, it was defined as a 'corridor'.

ISAF CASE BOOK, CASE NO.75

Chris Simon: Case No.75 in the *ISAF Case Book* looks at a situation where two boats were sailing downwind on opposite gybes to a leeward mark. In that situation, the jury's decision says the mark room that the port tack boat was required to give to the starboard tack boat was the space needed in existing conditions to sail promptly to the mark in a seamanlike way. That space was a direct corridor from the point where starboard entered the zone to a position close to and alongside the mark on the required side. So 'corridor' is a term that is actually used in that case.

Going around the left-hand gate mark

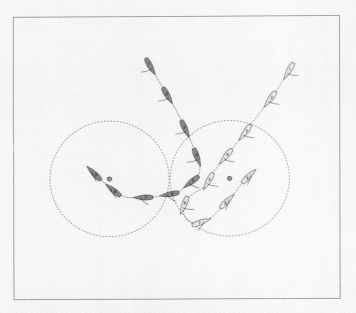

Chris: Now, the situation if two boats are approaching the left-hand mark of a leeward gate is worth a closer look. The boat on starboard is not obliged to gybe around the mark. If she wishes, the starboard boat can cause the port boat to gybe to avoid her, and then can sail her away from that mark. The starboard boat can then gybe and round that mark if she so wishes.

(Continued)

Asymmetric Sailing: Seems a bit unfair!

Chris: Well, it certainly creates tactical opportunities! If this was a single leeward mark, then the starboard boat would be obliged to gybe in the normal away around the mark. Rule 18.4 says she shall sail no further from the mark than her proper course to gybe. But where there is a leeward gate, Rule 18.4 doesn't apply.

Asymmetric Sailing: Strange that one rule should apply for a leeward mark, and another rule for a leeward gate . . .

Chris: An ISAF working party was tasked with coming up with a new mark rounding rule, but it was too difficult to come up with an appropriate form of words that was fair. So it's important for sailors to understand the distinction between leeward mark and leeward gate situations.

SEAMANLIKE ROUNDING

A seamanlike rounding is all you're entitled to. Mucking up your rounding is no defence

Asymmetric Sailing: Some asymmetric boats are very high performance and the boat handling can be very challenging. What's the definition of 'seamanlike' when you're talking about boats that are very hard to handle such as the 49er?

Chris: Well, 'seamanlike' is not a defined term within the Racing Rules and therefore we refer to its normal English meaning. I think one could say that its normal English meaning is that the boat is handled in a competent way, and again there are one or two cases which specifically say that if the boat isn't handled in a seamanlike way then from a rules point of view, giving room or keeping clear is not extended to cater for that lack of competence. So if a boat is by definition difficult to handle, then seamanlike does assume that the people who are sailing it are doing that competently. As soon as there is an implication or an admission that it was not done competently, then I think that begins to be unseamanlike. So you've got to look at seamanlike as being what you would expect in the upper end of the fleet – there's no concession for novices or short-handed sailors, for example.

Windward v Leeward Boat

Asymmetric Sailing: So let's say we've got blue boat sailing downwind with gennaker on starboard gybe. We've got yellow boat sailing upwind on starboard tack. Now yellow boat in all situations is the right-of-way boat, but the nature of asymmetrics is that they can change

This International 14 is struggling to keep clear of the boat coming upwind

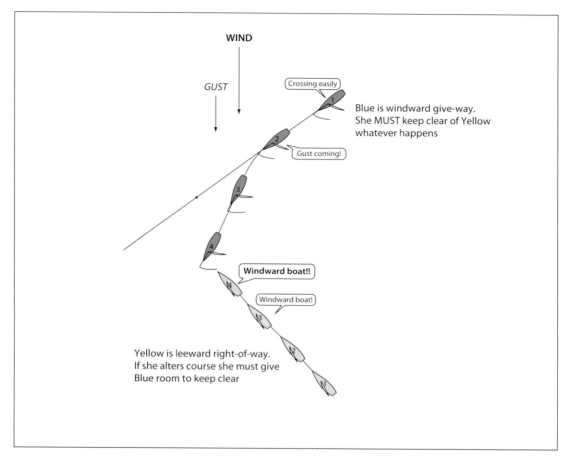

WIND

GUST

Crossing easily

Blue is windward give-way.
She MUST keep clear of Yellow
whatever happens

Gust coming!

Windward boat!!

Windward boat!

Yellow is leeward right-of-way.
If she alters course she must give
Blue room to keep clear

Windward v Leeward boats

course very quickly with even a slight change in wind speed. What sort of options does blue have if it suddenly gets hit by a gust and finds itself heading straight for yellow?

Chris: The only option is to keep clear, because that's what the rule demands. In this situation it's actually windward/leeward, Rule 11. Responding to a gust and keeping clear could be seen as a measure of seamanship. It is not a defence for a give-way boat to say: 'I was out of control, therefore I couldn't keep clear so I ought to be exonerated.' It's tough, simple as that. And blue in this scenario has no way out because she's on starboard, if she gybed onto port, it would give her a different angle and she'd probably get across, but it doesn't matter which way she does it – as long as she keeps clear.

Keeping a Lookout Downwind

Asymmetric Sailing: One of the problems is the lack of visibility with a lot of gennakers on modern day asymmetrics, so what is the advice other than keeping a good lookout?

Chris: There have been many discussions about this, but they have all led to the same conclusion, that it is the onus of the give-way boat. In fact it is the onus on *all* boats, to keep a proper lookout. A boat is not excused from keeping a proper lookout because she has a sail set in a particular way which means that she doesn't have good visibility in a particular direction.

Asymmetric Sailing: What about if you're going upwind and you see a boat coming towards you? What onus is there on you, if any, to highlight to the 'blind' boat that you're there?

Chris: Well I think it raises interesting questions because Rule 14, avoiding contact, actually says a boat shall avoid contact with another boat if reasonably possible; that includes keeping a proper lookout and doing everything that's reasonable and possible to avoid contact. There is a case that looks at such a situation, where there was contact between boats just before the start.

Planing fast, heeled over, on port gybe – this Melges crew had better be sure there's no one coming upwind on a collision course. . .

On each boat the bowman was involved in some sail handling and therefore neither bowman saw the other boat coming on a head-on collision course, and the boats did collide. The decision in that case was that neither boat would be exonerated because they didn't see the other boat. They were not doing everything that was reasonably possible to avoid the contact.

So going back to the situation you were talking about, I believe that a starboard tack boat coming upwind which sees a boat coming downwind with gennaker set towards her, irrespective of whether the other boat is on port gybe or starboard gybe, the starboard close-hauled boat would be well advised to hail. If there was a collision, even though she was the right-of-way boat and even though there's nothing in the rules to say she's got to hail, it might be argued that she didn't do all that was reasonably possible to avoid the collision. So the best advice for the close-hauled boat is to hail. Better safe than sorry.

Capsized Boat

Asymmetric Sailing: Let's say there are two boats on port, the lead boat gybed onto starboard, capsized and left the port boat nowhere to go. Who's in the right, who's in the wrong?

Chris: If we go back to basics, Rule 22 says if possible, a boat shall avoid a boat that is capsized or has not regained control after capsizing. So in this case the boat on port, if possible, shall

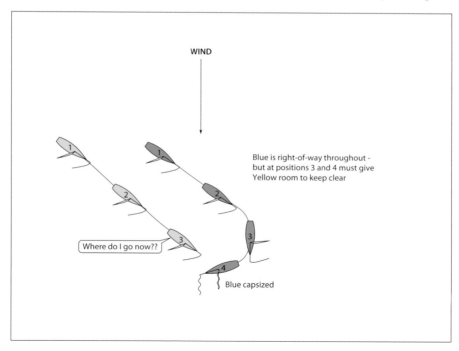

Capsized boat

avoid the boat that has capsized. The fact that she had already got onto starboard before she capsized is not actually relevant to the rules issue. So that assumes that the capsize happened when the other boat was far enough away to take avoiding action. If the capsize happens so close that it is not reasonably possible for the other boat to avoid the collision, then the upright boat will not have broken Rule 22.

Let's look in more detail at the timing of the incident. As soon as the lead boat gybed onto starboard, in other words as soon as her boom had travelled across the centre line, she became the right-of-way boat. Can one argue that a right-of-way boat that capsizes has changed course, in other words has she broken Rule 16? In this particular case she might also have broken Rule 15 because, irrespective of the capsize, her gybe was so close that the port tack boat couldn't take avoiding action, then she'd have broken Rule 15. This says she must give the right-of-way boat time and opportunity to change course; that is, she must initially give room. If, on the other hand, had she not capsized, the port boat could have avoided her and was only foiled by the boat that's now on starboard capsizing, then maybe it can be argued that she's broken Rule 16.

We don't have a case but we have a match racing call which says that a boat going ahead to going astern, or a boat that was going astern now going ahead is a change of course. So I don't think it's a very big step to go from that to saying that a boat that was sailing quickly across the bows of a give-way boat that capsizes and stops crossing the bows might also be argued to have changed course. We haven't actually got anything to rely on specifically there, but I believe that it's not an unreasonable extension of the match racing call.

Broaching in a Keelboat

Asymmetric Sailing: So dinghies and multihulls capsize, but keelboats broach. So a variation on the last question, let's say we're in SB20 keel boats which are quite capable of broaching and laying on their side after a gybe. So there are two boats on starboard gybe, and the lead boat – ahead and to windward – thinks that if she gybes successfully across will get clear ahead – but ends up laying on her side. Now this is a broach, the mast isn't in the water, but is a broach treated the same as a capsize in a dinghy?

Chris: No, I don't think it is, because Rule 22 says a boat is capsized when her masthead is in the water. However broaching is not a seamanlike manoeuvre so, again, it comes down to a question of distance and the ability of the right-of-way boat in this case to avoid her.

Asymmetric Sailing: So this boat can't just call starboard on a boat that's laid on its side?

Chris: No. She has got to take avoiding action because this is not to do with the right-of-way rules, this is coming back to Rule 14, the 'avoiding contact' rule. She has got to do what is reasonably possible to avoid contact, even though she's right-of-way. So it's a different rule but the outcome is the same. A boat that is under control has got to do all that is reasonably possible to avoid a boat that is not under control, whether it's capsized, broaching, mast fallen down, waterlogged, whatever.

Melges in mid-broach

Gybe-Set at the Windward Mark

Asymmetric Sailing: When you gybe-set at the windward mark on a typical port mark rounding, what rights if any do you have?

Chris: Firstly, the hoisting and setting of the gennaker has no relevance to the rules situation. Aside from any boats coming upwind towards the windward mark, a boat's main issue is likely to be with a boat that's following close behind her. Let's say the trailing boat was clear astern when the leading boat reached the zone; therefore the trailing boat has got to give the leading boat mark room (as she also would have to if she was overlapped outside her). There is no doubt that bearing away to a downwind course is her proper course around the mark. The question is, does gybing on to port count as part of her proper course around the mark? And I think the answer is yes, it is, provided it is done as a continuous manoeuvre. I think the only issue arises if the leading boat – having borne away to a downwind course on starboard – delays the gybe, so that she is now clearly past the mark. If she bears away, sails in a straight line for a little bit and then bears away further and gybes, that is not covered by her proper-course-at-the-mark rights. So during that gybe she would be going from right-of-way clear ahead to give-way port,

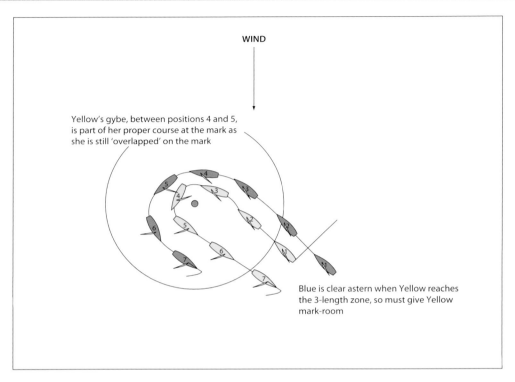

Yellow's gybe, between positions 4 and 5, is part of her proper course at the mark as she is still 'overlapped' on the mark

WIND

Blue is clear astern when Yellow reaches the 3-length zone, so must give Yellow mark-room

Gybing at the windward mark

and there it's not the action of the other boat that's caused the right-of-way to change, so she has no entitlement to room or anything else. If she is going to do that delayed gybe, she needs to keep clear throughout the manoeuvre.

Asymmetric Sailing: Let's say there's an offset mark a few boat lengths along from the windward mark – if the trailing boat has a slight overlap here, then the lead boat has no rights to gybe, right?

Chris: Again, the first question to ask is, were they overlapped at the zone of the offset mark? If they were overlapped at the zone, then the inside boat has all the control. If they were not overlapped in the zone then the trailing boat has got to give the leading boat mark room just as we discussed earlier.

Any rights while gybe-setting?

Asymmetric Sailing: In some fast boats like a 49er the best way to hoist the kite for a gybe-set is to hoist most of the kite first, and then gybe just as you've got the kite hoisted to the top of the mast. If you do this in stronger winds, you'd probably be out of the zone by the time you were gybing. So the question is, is it any defence for the lead boat to say I'm sailing my proper course because this is the way I'd gybe if I was on my own?

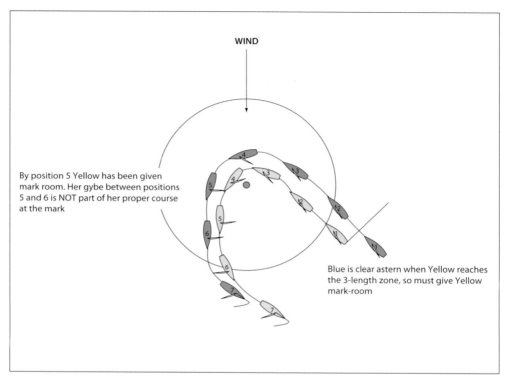

WIND

By position 5 Yellow has been given mark room. Her gybe between positions 5 and 6 is NOT part of her proper course at the mark

Blue is clear astern when Yellow reaches the 3-length zone, so must give Yellow mark-room

Gybing after the windward mark

Chris: No, because the definition of mark room says 'room to sail her proper course while at the mark'. So, if in this scenario, she is clearly no longer at the mark because she's now one or two boat lengths beyond it, mark room has switched off. You're back in the land of normal right-of-way rules and, irrespective of whether or not the kite is up, her gybe will take her onto port and she will go from right-of-way starboard to give-way port. She's got no protection under Rule 15. She's got to keep clear all the time, from the moment the boom crosses the centre line.

Two Sails Against Three Sails on a Reach

Asymmetric Sailing: Some classes like the International 14 have reaches in their race courses, and there's sometimes a decision about whether or not to carry a gennaker down to the gybe mark. So let's say there's one International 14 with a gennaker up, but with a rival to leeward without gennaker, two-sail reaching to the mark. Talk us through the potential issues in this scenario.

Chris: The two-sail boat is the leeward boat, the three-sail boat has established an overlap up to windward so there is no doubt the leeward boat has luffing rights, and that Rule 17 does not

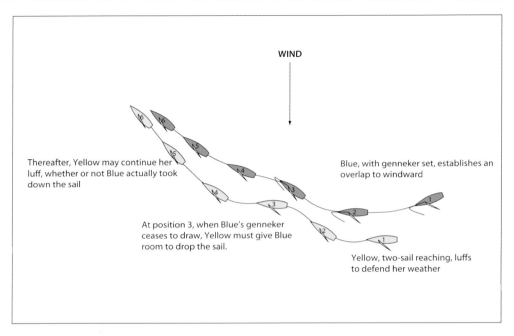

WIND

Thereafter, Yellow may continue her luff, whether or not Blue actually took down the sail

Blue, with genneker set, establishes an overlap to windward

At position 3, when Blue's genneker ceases to draw, Yellow must give Blue room to drop the sail.

Yellow, two-sail reaching, luffs to defend her weather

Two sails against three sails

apply. She will be the right-of-way boat when they're overlapped, the leeward right-of-way boat altering course. So a right-of-way boat altering course has got to give room for the other boat to keep clear. I don't think we have got a case about it, but we've got a match racing call about it. The match racing call says that the leeward boat can luff, but at the point where the windward boat's genneker ceases to draw, the leeward boat has then got to give some extra room for the windward boat to drop the genneker. If the windward boat drops her genneker then the leeward boat can continue to luff. If the windward boat, having been given the room, does not drop the genneker, the leeward boat can also continue to luff without making any extra allowance. And I think it's the same here, so the leeward boat can certainly luff until the windward boat's genneker is flapping. At that stage she must make sure that there is sufficient room for the windward boat to take down the genneker if that's what she wants to do. But I suspect, in most asymmetric boats, by the time it gets to that point, the leeward boat will have moved ahead of the windward boat anyway.

Handicap Racing – Different Boats at the Same Mark

Asymmetric Sailing: In handicap racing, with boats of different speeds and sizes competing against each other, tell us about the rights and wrongs of a scenario where, say, an 18-foot skiff is closing rapidly on a mark where a 10-foot Mirror dinghy is about to enter the three-boat length zone. How is the size of the boat length zone defined, for example?

Chris: The zone is defined as the area around the mark within a distance of three hull lengths of the boat nearer to it. So, if a slow Mirror is approaching a mark, the zone is three Mirror lengths because the Mirror is the boat that's closer. As soon as the longer boat – in this case the 18-foot skiff – gets ahead, the zone is three of her hull lengths. So they go from not being in the zone of the short boat to instantaneously being well inside the zone of the long boat. Because they never 'reach' the zone we do not have that reference point to use rule 18.2(b) – so the basic rule 18.2(a) applies and the outside boat must give the inside boat mark-room.

Bowsprit in 'Normal Position'

Asymmetric Sailing: How does having a bowsprit extended out of the front of the boat affect overlaps for rules situations?

Chris: An overlap is determined by equipment in normal position. The definition says that one boat is clear astern of another when her hull and equipment *in normal position* are behind a line abeam of the aftermost point of the other boat's hull and equipment in normal position. So if we think of two International 14s approaching a windward mark and one boat is clear of astern of the other. If the boat astern then pulls out her bowsprit she doesn't create an overlap because having your bowsprit out on an upwind leg is not equipment in normal position.

Bowsprits on SB20s need to be retracted when not being used to fly the gennaker

Asymmetric Sailing: In some classes like the SB20 there are specific rules about when you're allowed to extend your bowsprit, in terms of when you're permitted to extend it in preparation for a gennaker hoist on a spacer leg, for example. But if you're in a class where there aren't specific rules, how do you determine 'normal position' for a bowsprit?

Chris: Well, let's say there was a protest between two boats where, on a spacer leg, one boat had pulled its bowsprit out half way along the spacer leg, and claimed an overlap at the offset mark, it would be up to that boat to produce evidence that this was the normal way of sailing those boats. Equally, the other boat would say: 'Well, I didn't pull mine out until I was two lengths from the offset mark and that is the norm.' The argument would really revolve around that. But, again, my experience of people judging – including my own – three length zones are so grey it would be awfully difficult to reach a conclusion. Probably the best way of determining whether the bowsprit is in normal position or not is by bringing in expert witnesses, top sailors in the class, and asking them how and when they set their bowsprits during the offset leg.

Gybing a Fully-Battened Mainsail Without Upsetting the Umpires

Asymmetric Sailing: In light winds, gybing a fully-battened mainsail such as you have on the majority of asymmetric boats can be quite difficult, because it can be hard convincing the

Light air gybing in a Melges 24

battens to flick from one gybe to another. From a rules perspective, what sort of things do sailors need to be aware of when they're gybing the battens on their sail?

Chris: It is a matter of whether the tug on the mainsheet creates an effect that could be interpreted as pumping under Rule 42, the propulsion rule. If, in attempting to gybe the battens, there is a quick flick so that the boom doesn't move significantly and all that happens is that the battens flip across up the sail, then that does not have any effect, or its effect is negligible. So it doesn't break the rule. On the other hand, if the pull on the mainsheet moves the boom a significant amount, and the whole sail moves as well – the fact that the battens pop across in the course of that happening would not exonerate you from pumping if it had an effect on the boat.

In the British National Match Racing Championship, racing the J/80 keelboat in light winds there's often a problem with the top batten inverting. It's not a fully-battened sail but the top batten spans the full width of the sail. As umpires we normally tell the competitors in that situation that they are allowed one flick to try and gybe the batten. But if that fails they must then find some other way of doing it, which may be a downward pull on the sail, either via the cunningham or directly pulling on the boom itself. So if they have their flick and the batten doesn't gybe and we don't see any effect on the boat's motion, then we let that one go, but they're not allowed a second try. Obviously this is going to vary a lot from boat to boat, and also with the umpires you're dealing with, so it's important to clarify this grey area before a major championship.

CHAPTER 10

THE FINAL FIVE PER CENT

No matter what level you're at, there is always room for improvement. In this chapter we'll look at how to make those crucial, incremental improvements to your boat, your equipment, and yourself. Small changes can make massive differences to your results, and the most successful sailors are those that pay the most attention to the tiniest details.

Perfecting Your Equipment

It would be easy to write a whole book on this subject. Instead we'll focus on a few key points.

The main point to bear in mind is that attention to detail makes a massive difference in high-performance boats. When you're juggling the tiller, mainsheet, kite sheets all while balancing on the edge of the boat on the trapeze, the last thing you want to have to cope with

Attention to small details can make massive differences on the race course

is a cleat that won't hold the sheet properly or anything else that distracts you from actually sailing the boat. Small things can lead to a capsize, and a capsize can lead to gear damage. So pay attention to the details.

The best place to start is to look at the national champion's boat, or the most competent sailor in your local fleet. With their permission, copy their rope lengths and anything else that you see done differently on their boat.

Here are a few examples of things that might help improve the smooth running of your boat:

- **Tapered gennaker halyard**: The only bit of the halyard that needs to be thick is the bit you hold during the hoist. Everything else can be as thin as possible for the given strength required. On a 49er, for example, you might have 3mm spectra from the head of the kite all the way to where it's about to go into the halyard cleat. From this point on it can thicken out to 5mm, good for gripping the cleat and good for gripping with your hands.
- **Loop on the gennaker sheet**: Instead of tying your gennaker sheets on to the clew of the kite with separate knots, use a loop in the centre of the sheets, creating a smooth run past the forestay. Anything you can do to reduce friction as the kite goes through the gybe will help speed up the manoeuvre.
- **Tapered kite sheets**: These can help the kite set more easily on light winds, weighing down the clew less than if you use thick, non-tapered sheets.
- **Lubricating spray**: Spray anywhere on the boat where you want to reduce unwanted friction. I use McLube but there are other brands available. It's not cheap, but spraying the

The kite sheets on the left could catch on the forestay during a gybe, whereas the smooth run on the kite sheets on the right will make for a more reliable gybe

chute mouth, the bowsprit and other parts of the hoist system can make it much easier to get the kite up and down. Just make sure you don't spray the parts of the boat where you're going to be treading, because these lube sprays can be super-slippery underfoot.

- **Vital spares**: Always take a few spare shackles, pieces of string and other things that you might need in an emergency. For trapeze boats, think about taking a spare tiller extension with you. If you break one, you'll certainly struggle to continue racing without it, and it might make it difficult to get home safely. Carbon tiller extensions weigh very little, so it's worth the small weight penalty for the added peace of mind.

Lubricating spray to reduce friction in the gennaker hoist system and chute

How often to a buy new kite?

On a lot of asymmetric boats, gennakers don't really get much slower as they get older. At least not in a straight line. But, over time, as the cloth loses its shiny, water-resistant coating, and becomes porous and prone to soaking up water, you'll find it becomes harder to handle through the manoeuvres. The kite

Tight-luffed, highly-loaded gennakers – such as on this Tornado – need regular replacement. But more lightly-loaded kites can last a couple of seasons

might stick to the jib through gybes, or get a lot harder to hoist and drop into the chute. When to buy a replacement kite really depends on how much your manoeuvres are being affected by your old kite. Really high-performance multihulls with tight-luffed gennakers need to replace their sails more often as the shape becomes distorted, but for lower-performance asymmetrics, a new kite should last you for a year's worth of weekend racing.

DARREN BUNDOCK, KEEPING IT SIMPLE

A lot of people like trapeze height adjusters, but on small cats like the Tornado and F18, we just use Ronstan 'dogbones', which are basically set and forget. We generally set ourselves for the day, adjust the bowline for whether you want to be up or down a bit. But I really hate adjustable trapezes. There's always something going wrong with them. It's always at the wrong height. With the dogbones, when you get out on trapeze, you can just get sailing straight away. There isn't time to be mucking around with adjusting stuff. We have very few ropes, and the ropes we do have are always cut to the minimum length.

Team Work and Communication

One of the hardest things to get right in high-performance sailing boats is efficient communication and understanding between the crew. Because the boat is demanding to sail and it travels at a rapid rate, typically around a short course, the decision making comes thick and fast.

Iker Martinez and Xabi Fernandez have sailed together for years, a major contributing factor to their Olympic and World titles in the 49er

A Nacra team working in perfect harmony

Practise your set moves and build up a few standard forms of communication to that you can reduce chatter to a minimum. The fastest boats also tend to be the quietest. Calibrate sail controls so that you can make adjustments with the minimum of guess work. Instead of saying 'ease the vang a bit', it's a lot easier for everyone to understand 'ease the vang to 4', for example.

When your crew mate isn't quite doing what you want them to do, say, maybe they're standing too far forwards, choose your words carefully. Tell them what you want, not what you don't want. Instead of saying, 'You're standing too far forwards', give them a more specific instruction like 'Step back six inches'.

These things are hard to get right straight away, but the important thing is to agree to offer each other constructive feedback on what each of you think is working, and what could be done better. Try not to get stuck into making too many corrections at once, or during an already busy sailing session, but remember the main points and discuss them in a debrief once you're back on shore.

Expert Advice

Who makes the decisions?

ISAF Youth Champion in the 29er skiff, Frances Peters talks about tactical decision-making in the team.

Asymmetric Sailing: Frances, what's the main difference in communication style between racing a slower boat and a faster asymmetric skiff like the 29er?

Frances: One of the biggest transitions probably was the amount of communication needed from the crew downwind, to constantly be feeding back how much pressure they have in the kite. This feedback enables the helm to ease the boat down every wave, as low as they can get without losing pressure in the gennaker completely. That was a big transition and really important in team building of course, because the communication is absolutely vital.

With the crew focused on kite trim, tactical decisions downwind should be taken by the helm

(Continued)

Asymmetric Sailing: What about the split of responsibilities downwind? Who's calling the tactics, for example?

Frances: I think tactics is the helm's job. It's really important that the crew focuses entirely on the kite because their job downwind is to make sure that the kite stays filling, feeding back how much pressure they've got in the kite and possibly helping with pumping and ooching down the waves. The helm is responding to the feedback they're getting from the crew and they're looking around, calling in the pressure, calling in where the other boats are and generally doing all the tactics and strategy.

Asymmetric Sailing: One of the toughest parts of the course is the leeward gate, where the decision-making process can change depending on what's going on around you. How do you manage that, and communicate your plans to the crew?

Frances: Well, just talk lots! Don't try and tell them what's going on I'd say, because you generally haven't got time to do that, so you've just got to make sure that you tell them what to do with as much opportunity as possible. Coming into a gate mark I generally try and say in advance, 'okay, it's going to be a gybe drop here', for example, and my crew will instantly know what that means and what that entails. I'll try to give them an idea of what I think the situation will be but, as you say, situations do change. In which case I'd say it's the crew's responsibility to keep up with the helm and it's the helm's responsibility to feed in as much information as they possibly can and give the crew time. You can't afford to be vague and you can't afford to assume that the crew knows what's going on. It's about teamwork, it's lots of practice. Whatever call you make in any situation, both of you have to know what's involved because you've practised it so many times before.

Team work in a sportsboat

Brian Hutchinson talks about the make-up of a typical team in the Melges 24, and managing the communication between the crew. . .

Asymmetric Sailing: Like a lot of keelboats, there is a maximum crew weight limit on the Melges 24, which seems that you end up with either five little or four big people. Which is best?

Brian: If you have a couple of small people in the group then you're probably going to go to five up, and the small people better be strong. We sailed the 2003 Worlds in San Francisco [which Brian won crewing for 13-year-old Shark Khan]. I actually like sailing with four, but then I had to have three big guys sailing with me because

I weigh 70kg, and there's more elbow room on a four person crew, of course. One of the benefits of a four is you all fit in the same rental car and two rooms in a hotel! It's a lot easier getting around. But generally, in a four person crew, you're not going to have women on board because you all have to be fairly big.

Asymmetric Sailing: So you fit in one car, but you've got no female company, so there are pros and cons here!

Brian: Yeah! Generally in a five-person car, if the fifth person is a woman then there's always room, right? On a Melges there are two positions that you don't have to be super-powerful, and so somebody of smaller stature – whether male or female – can handle those positions. You can actually sail the boat with three although certain jobs get kind of left – you're not sailing as cleanly, perhaps. People have sailed with three, but that's rare.

Asymmetric Sailing: What tips do you have for managing the flow of communication between the crew?

(Continued)

Train hard, fight easy

Brian: Well I've done it in many different ways. I have an architectural background so I'm open to trying all sorts of things. I think it works for most groups to have a fairly quiet boat. In fact, I much prefer a quiet boat. It's easy for the noise level to get too high, and some of the comments are more accurate than others and are more useful than others. It's really best to train a lot and then when you go into the race it's more of a walk.

Asymmetric Sailing: The old Japanese motto of, 'train hard, fight easy'. . .

Brian: Yeah, I think that's the case. Everyone knows what they're supposed to do, so there's less of that kind of chatter about mechanics, and then there's less chatter about little tweaks – how we should be set up and that sort of thing. It's nice if you can get a lot of time on the water. So when it comes to the racing we can just enjoy a beautiful day on the water, and so the focus should be mainly on the wind and your position relative to the fleet, and possibly a mode change or your performance with your mode and set-up.

It's best to have, perhaps, one voice on the boat – and that's the tactician – with an occasional back-and-forth between tactician and helmsman, and perhaps somebody whose eyes are on the horizon. Just an occasional comment, maybe limited to just a few comments per leg, so it's fairly mellow, fairly quiet and so we're all focused on what really has to happen. The tactician can be a real talker, and that's okay if everybody's into it, or they can be really quiet. Like when I sailed with Mark Reynolds [multiple Olympic medallist] the guy would maybe comment three times on the beat, and that was just once for each tack. Richard Clarke [Finn Olympian and Volvo Ocean Race winner] was a little more talkative but he's very creative and very observant, and it's good to see that stuff, so people can follow the movie. I mean, it's really bad to have the bow person hanging over the lifeline like a bat and not even involved in what's going on. I think everybody should be involved so everybody's tuned in to how we're sailing the boat.

Jonathan McKee [another Olympic Champion and Melges 24 World Champion] also talks very little on the boat and they all know what they're doing. If you're on a boat where everybody is a good helmsperson and good sailor in their own right on singlehanded boats, and we all pretty much know what we're trying to do here. If we're seeing the development of a wind shift or velocity change or a condition, or coming into a fleet – if we're going to try to lead back. We all know whether we're about to tack because it's obvious, we're going to lead back to the weather mark or wherever that may be. So it's kind of nice if you're all tuned in and just sharp. It keeps you awake, too, if you're maybe not involved in those decisions and you're on the rail, we all know that we're all hiking just before the powerful roll, all doing that kind of stuff, so the body language takes care of a lot of it.

Goal Setting - Do This and You Will Always Improve

I wrote this section in conjunction with Richard Parslow, a world champion sailor and my former RYA coach when I was racing the 49er.

Of all the things that full-time, professional sailors do that the rest of us weekend warriors do not do, structured goal setting is probably the most important. Fortunately, it is also one of the less demanding activities (compared to, say, completing a hundred perfect tacks). With the right approach it can be done quickly – and it can even be fun.

Goal-setting is one of the cheapest and most effective tools at your disposal

Why goal setting makes a difference

It's not just about the time and money (and energy!) you have available, it's how you spend those resources. For example, practising some boathandling exercises might be a better use of a day's sailing than doing a couple of club races. Or maybe a day's coaching is a better investment than buying a new jib.

Think about what you want to achieve, then set some specific goals. Goal setting has been shown to be a major factor in improving performance in almost every area of life; yet most of us still do not set any goals, let alone reach them. Maybe we are protecting ourselves: if we do not set goals we cannot fail at them! But that is lazy thinking and it brings only frustration.

So let's look at setting some sailing goals – and working out how to achieve them.

Mapping out your road to success

Think about your long-term sailing goals. How exactly do you want to improve? What specific goal will motivate you to do everything you need to do to achieve it? Maybe you want to be so fit and skilled that you are 'at one with your boat' in all conditions; or maybe you just want to be able to compete in 25 knots without capsizing.

Try to stick to Performance and Process goals: those that depend entirely on your own efforts and abilities. You *can* set Outcome goals: winning a club series or a championship – or even an Olympic medal. But you have to accept that achieving such goals is not completely within your control.

You want to improve as much as possible with the talent, time and money you bring to the game, so aim high. Describe your goal in inspirational terms and write it down somewhere as your Main Goal. Once you know where you are going, you can start to work out how to get there. What's most important in the goal-setting process is the journey you take to reach the desired outcome.

You can do quite a lot on paper – as long as you keep it somewhere safe and easily accessible. I use Goalscape software (www.goalscape.com) because it can capture an entire campaign in a single picture – and because it's really easy to use.

Lots of sailors in Olympic classes use this tool, but it can help anyone who is serious about improving their skills – and results.

Next year's results depend on what you do right now

The best way to plan your route to your main goal is to break down your sailing into different areas and work out exactly what you need to do in each.

The fundamental 'building blocks' are always the same, whatever your current abilities and whatever your goals. In the diagram below you can see the top-level subgoals around the main goal in the centre. (The size of each subgoal's slice represents its relative importance.)

Three of these goals are about arriving at the starting line in the best possible shape:

1. Logistics (planning the year: training, events, travel and accommodation, etc.)
2. Gear (hull, rig, sails, foils, fittings, clothing, etc.)
3. Budget (money available for equipment, events etc.)

These goals are all about preparation. You can start thinking right now about what you need to do and how to do it.

The other three are about the abilities you need when racing:

1. Boathandling (executing every skill in all conditions)
2. Finding the best course (strategy and tactics)
3. Fitness (mental skills, physical strength, balance, etc)

These are the core goals for maximising your performance on the water

Define specific goals in each area and plan exactly how you are going to achieve them. Break down each subgoal area into further subgoals. Keep breaking down the subgoals even further until you have defined specific actions to achieve them all. Below is a detail view of the 'Boathandling' area, showing the key aspects of boathandling that you need to master in order to race properly and the specific manoeuvres involved.

Focus your efforts

When you first do a proper goal setting exercise, it can be exciting when you see all the different areas where you can improve. It can also be overwhelming! A common mistake here is to go from doing nothing to trying to do too much all at once.

A good way to start is to identify a maximum of three areas that offer the greatest opportunity for improving your performance. How do you do that? One way is to think back through your last season, or even your last race. Be honest: what did you do well and what let you down? Where could you make the greatest improvements in the shortest time? If you capsized a lot when tacking in strong winds for example, you have an easy answer.

So if you can come up with three ideas for tacking more safely, then you can write them into your tacking process breakdown as sub-goals:

1. Ease sails sooner before the tack.
2. Steer more slowly through the tack.
3. Move more quickly up to the new windward side.

Work out some good ways to practise and how to measure your progress. If you train in a pair or a group, watch what the others do. Ask them to watch you and give you some specific feedback.

On the other hand if your boathandling is good but your race strategy is poor, look at your information-gathering and decision-making processes.

Find out how other people do all this stuff: talk to some of the good guys – or visit a sailing forum. Debrief thoroughly after each practice or competition. Be positive: agree where you have improved and how much. Update your written plan – seeing your progress increases your motivation and highlights what you need to prioritise next.

If you identify specific problems in every area and find three possible solutions for each of them (or just one!), you are already doing better than 95% of your opposition.

Stick at it!

Persist with this process of gradual, incremental improvements to the key areas of your game and your weaknesses will start to disappear. You may find that your old failings become your new strengths: each is a separate proof of the effectiveness of your process.

Soon you will enjoy doing the very things that you used to mess up. If you were nervous in strong winds you will be more competent and more confident: you will love racing in a breeze when you can stay upright while your rivals are falling over.

Olympic Champion Iain Percy once said: 'I enjoy the process of improvement almost more than the winning itself. That's where the real satisfaction comes. Identify your weaknesses, set goals, practise until you get better, and the results will look after themselves.'

So, start setting some goals for your sailing right now. It is the single activity most likely to improve your performance and results; there is simply no excuse not to do it. And don't stop goal setting even if you reach your goals – in fact *especially* if you reach your goals. Instead, set yourself new goals in every area – and start working on them today.

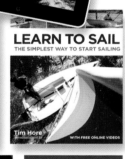

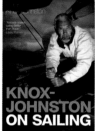
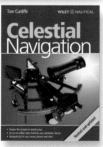